Essential Hindi Grammar

Essential Hindi Grammar

With Examples from Modern Hindi Literature

CHRISTINE EVERAERT

University of Hawai'i Press
Honolulu

Printed in the United States of America

22 21 20 19 18 17 6 5 4 3 2 1

Library of Congress Cataloging-in-Publication Data

Names: Everaert, Christine, author.
Title: Essential Hindi grammar : with examples from modern Hindi literature / Christine Everaert.
Description: Honolulu : University of Hawai‘i Press, [2017] | Includes bibliographical references and index.
Identifiers: LCCN 2016037832 | ISBN 9780824857875 (cloth ; alk. paper) | ISBN 9780824871857 (pbk. ; alk. paper)
Subjects: LCSH: Hindi language—Grammar.
Classification: LCC PK1933 .E94 2017 | DDC 491.4/35—dc23
LC record available at https://lccn.loc.gov/2016037832

University of Hawai‘i Press books are printed on acid-free paper and meet the guidelines for permanence and durability of the Council on Library Resources.

Designed by Wanda China

Contents

List of Tables

Preface

This book is not designed to be a language course. It should be seen as an additional tool that will allow language students from all levels, as well as researchers of linguistics, to find answers about Modern Standard Hindi grammar in an independent and systematic way. A descriptive grammar is an indispensable tool for the beginning student of written and spoken Hindi, as well as for the advanced student who also wants to read literary Hindi, and those who teach Hindi as a second language at the college level. This concise and comprehensive grammar aims at encouraging students to truly learn the language in all its complexity, allowing them to analyze texts they have never read before. Because each grammatical topic is illustrated not only with some basic examples, but also with more complex examples from modern literature that are often omitted from textbooks or teach-yourself courses, it satisfies the need for a research tool for advanced students and scholars of modern Hindi literature and media texts.

Grammatical concepts and terminology are introduced and explained from scratch in this book. The purpose of this is twofold: in Europe, most learners of Hindi have already studied (multiple) other languages, or students are studying Sanskrit alongside Hindi. While the setup of the grammar will help those experienced language students with their study of Hindi, it is written in such a way that it makes sure not to alienate the student who is new to language learning. The wording in this grammar is simple and plain, but it teaches the student basic grammatical terminology, without feeling oversimplified to the more advanced scholar. For the convenience of scholars, grammatical terminology is also provided in Hindi, so they can consult grammars in Hindi or use the grammar if they want to study Hindi in India, where Sanskrit grammatical terminology is traditionally used when teaching Hindi. Scientific transliteration is provided consistently throughout the book, wherever Hindi in Devanagari is presented.

This grammar consists of three parts. Part I offers a short introduction to the linguistic background and development of Modern Standard Hindi, and its special relationship to Urdu. Part II deals with the Devanagari alphabet and everything related to its script, spelling, and pronunciation. While modern social media often use Romanagari—that is, Hindi in the Roman alphabet—knowledge of the Devanagari alphabet is indispensable for anybody who wants to gain access to literature and primary sources in Hindi. The alphabet is introduced in the way it was organized by the grammarian Panini, well over two thousand years ago, drawing attention to the place and way of articulation of each letter. This helps Hindi students to correctly pronounce sounds that are foreign to them. Part III, consisting of twelve chapters, presents the actual grammar. Chapter I explains the use of cases and postpositions. Chapters II through IV deal with everything related to nouns, adjectives, and pronouns. Syntax and word order is discussed in chapter V. Special sentence structures to express obligations, experiencing feelings and emotions, as well as the verb "to have," relative-correlative, and superlative/comparative constructions can be found in this chapter as well. Chapters VI and VII are dedicated to verbal conjugations: all existing simple and compound tenses are explained in chapter VI, while chapter VII deals with the vector verbs used in Hindi. Chapter VIII focuses on the use of participles as adjectives and nouns, as well as their predicative and adverbial use. Chapter IX offers an insight in morphology and includes a list of common prefixes and suffixes. In chapters X through XII, echo words, numbers, and time telling are analyzed.

Every grammatical topic is illustrated with a number of example sentences. The more complex examples have been taken from seven modern short stories, written by important Hindi writers. All the examples are presented in the Devanagari script, followed by the transliteration. The name of the author, placed between brackets following the example, indicates from which text the example has been taken. The following seven texts were used, listed alphabetically by the name of the author:

सिद्दीक़ी साहब (*siddīqī sāhab*) by Abdul Bismillāh[1]
लालू बंदर, नथ्थु मगरमछ (*lālū bandar, naththu magarmach*) by Gulzār[2]
कफ़न (*kafan*) by Premcand[3]
मलबे का मालिक (*malbe kā mālik*) by Mohan Rākeś[4]
दिल्ली की बात (*dillī kī bāt*) by Pāṇḍey Becan Śarmā 'Ugra'[5]
प्रेज़ेण्ट्स (*prezeṇṭs*) by Bhagvatīcaraṇ Varmā[6]
दुखी-दुखी! (*dukhī-dukhī*) by Yaśpāl[7]

The short story by Gulzār has been included primarily because it offers important, common examples from colloquial Hindi, and not just the standard written language. The text is a reworked *Pañcatantra* story, in which the main characters are animals, offering some special examples and grammatical features.

* * * * *

No book is the result of just one person's labor. I want to express my indebtedness to Richard Delacy, Harvard University, for providing me with valuable comments and feedback. His input made the end result a better book. In the final stages of revising the manuscript, Fulbright Language Teaching Assistant Charulika Dhawan, University of Delhi, made a valuable contribution by helping to design example sentences and providing numerous examples and feedback that allowed me to more accurately describe some grammatical rules and peculiarities. Fulbright Language Teaching Assistant Sadaf Hussain, Aligarh University, provided similar feedback in an earlier stage of the preparation of the book manuscript.

In a more informal way, numerous students provided feedback, often without realizing it, every time they asked a question or made a mistake. This book is in part the fruit of their labor as well. In the

1. Bismillāh, *Atithi devo bhav*, 19–28.
2. Gulzār, *Rāvī pār aur anya kahāniyāṃ*, 37–41.
3. Premcand, *Mānsarovar 1*, 179–199.
4. Rākeś, *Mohan rākeś kī sampurṇ kahāniyāṃ*, 346–349.
5. Ugra, *Aisī holī khelo lāl*, 26–33.
6. Varmā, *Merī priy kahāniyāṃ*, 58–64.
7. Yaśpāl, *Yaśpāl kī sampūrṇ kahāniyāṃ*, 46–49.

final stages of revision, Connor Houghton, Amber Robb, and Nicole Fox, (former) students of University of Utah, Salt Lake City, donated their time by proofreading the manuscript, both in Hindi and English, at various (often inconvenient) points in time. Apart from this, they also offered me their invaluable friendship, which has been an equally important contribution to the production of this book. I want to thank *mere jaan* in particular, for his continuous friendship and support.

Abbreviations and Symbols Used

x > y	x becomes y
x < y	x is derived from y
Abl.	ablative
absol.	absolutive
Acc.	accusative
adj.	adjective
adv.	adverb
cont.	continuous
def.	definite
D.O.	direct object
f.	feminine
fut.	future
hon.	honorific
imper.	imperative
impfct.	imperfective
indef.	indefinite
indir.	indirect
Instr.	instrumental
lit.	literally
Loc.	locative
m.	masculine
MOS	masculine oblique singular
neg.	negation
Nom.	nominative
Obl.	oblique
part.	participle
perfct.	perfective
pl.	plural
ppn.	postposition
pred.	predicate
Prk.	Prakrits
prs.	present
sg.	singular
Skt.	Sanskrit
Subj.	subjunctive
Voc.	vocative

PART I

Hindi: A Brief Introduction

I. LINGUISTIC BACKGROUND AND EVOLUTION

Hindi, like English, is a language within the Indo-European or Indo-Germanic family.[1] To be more specific, Hindi belongs to the New Indo-Aryan (NIA) subgroup and descends from Sanskrit, an Old Indo-Aryan (OIA) language. It is important to bear in mind, however, that even though Hindi is an Indo-European language, it has been profoundly affected by several other languages, of both Indo-European and non-Indo-European origins. Thus, one should not underestimate the influence of Persian (Indo-European), Arabic (Semitic), Portuguese (Indo-European), Turkish (Turkic), or English, all of which contributed significantly to the Hindi lexicon.

Today, modern Hindi is composed using the Devanagari script. As noted in article 343 of the Constitution of India, "Hindi in Devanagari script is the official language of the Union."[2] While the history and time line of the development of this script is complicated and not without controversy, most scholars agree that Devanagari, as we know it today, was widely used in South Asia by the tenth century. Since that time, it has been used to write well over one hundred languages, including the classical and contemporary languages of Sanskrit, Hindi, Nepali, and Marathi.[3]

I.1. EVOLUTION OF MODERN STANDARD HINDI

Languages develop and evolve over many centuries. Although this process can be quite complicated, with many different mechanisms in play, concrete aspects of Hindi's development, from its earliest usage to its current application, can be seen upon investigation. To begin with, the language's connection to Sanskrit is visible in a variety of grammatical and lexical elements. Through the instrument of simplification, Hindi engaged with Sanskrit, whereby it gradually

1. This part is based on Everaert, *Tracing the Boundaries*, 231–279; Masica, *Indo-Aryan Languages*, 25–75, 133–184.
2. "Constitution of India 1949," accessed on October 22, 2015, http://indiankanoon.org/doc/379861/.
3. "The Script Source," accessed on October, 26, 2015, http://scriptsource.org/scr/Deva, Masica, *Indo-Aryan Languages*, 133–150.

leveled cases and assimilated consonant clusters. Another feature of Hindi's evolution highlights the fact that its speakers came into contact with speakers of other languages. During the centuries over which Modern Standard Hindi developed, Hindi speakers interacted with peoples of numerous cultures, each of whom left their linguistic mark to various degrees. In the next section, we will take a more detailed look at some of the languages that greatly impacted the transformation of the Hindi language.

I.1.1. SIMPLIFICATION

Just like knowledge of Latin can be valuable for students of French or Italian, students who have studied Sanskrit, whether Vedic or Classical, will find that their knowledge can be applied to learning Hindi, as the two languages are closely related. Between the third and seventh centuries B.C., in the "golden age" of Sanskrit literature, the South Asian grammarian Panini compiled nearly four thousand rules, creating a grammar of Classical Sanskrit, often credited as being the oldest grammar in the world. This language that he standardized included a rather complex grammar that reflected qualities of an even older Vedic Sanskrit, both of which proved too complicated for everyday usage by the masses. Thus, believed by many to have been the medium of only educated Hindu men, Classical Sanskrit was strongly connected to Hindu liturgy, never being a truly spoken language. In contrast, vernacular and regional dialects, referred to as Prakrits, displayed heightened simplification and modification of Sanskrit and subsequently arose in prominence between 500 B.C. and A.D. 1100. These Prakrits (i.e., Middle Indo-Aryan languages) are often considered the languages of the people, as they were used in common daily life, in direct opposition to Classical Sanskrit, which was the literary language reserved for elite adherents of Hinduism. After Prakrits gained importance over the course of several centuries, and as religious communities came to select different Prakrits as vehicles for religious writings (Pali for Buddhists, Ardhamagadhi Prakrit for Jains, etc.), these languages underwent a further process of simplification and change. As such, New Indo-Aryan languages, like Hindi, Urdu, Bengali, and Panjabi, began to emerge around A.D. 1000. Links between the different forms of Sanskrit, Prakrits, and Hindi are evident to any student of those languages.[4]

I.1.2. CULTURAL AND LINGUISTIC INFLUENCE OF POLITICAL EVENTS

When one examines the evolution of a given language, its exposure to and interaction with other communities and cultures is a distinct factor by which important linguistic changes are generated. Hindi's development was no exception. Because India was strategically located, with an abundance of natural resources, the region and its languages experienced an extensive history of international engagement. Unfortunately, such illustrious qualities also made India attractive to foreign rulers who wanted to establish their power over the vast territory.

Undoubtedly, one of the more well-known periods, which left a strong influence on Hindi, was Muslim rule over northern India, whereby parts of North and Central India were dominated by Central-Asian Muslim rulers from the eleventh century until 1707.

Beginning in the seventh and eight centuries, Islam, and with it Arabic, spread across a large region from Spain to Persia, eventually encompassing most of Central Asia, up to the Chinese border. Throughout these early years of Islam, all Muslim troops were Arabs, and as such Arabic was introduced to this broad territory. However, in the East, in Iran and Central Asia, Arabic culture was unable to supplant the native language of Pehlavi, or Middle Persian. Instead, Arabic merely interacted with Middle Persian, upon which a ninth-century Arabicized variant emerged, to be named New Persian or Farsi. By the tenth century, this new language was in standard use, being the preferred medium for literature and communication. Thus, within three centuries, Arabic in Iran had to yield its place of importance to Farsi.[5]

Meanwhile, in the same period, the Persian army came to include many Central Asian generals who spoke Turkic languages as their

4. Deshpande, *Efforts*, 218–229; Pollock, *Language of the Gods*, 39–51.
5. Versteegh, *Arabic*, 71.

mother tongue. Because of this multiethnic military composition, some Turkish words were incorporated into the Arabicized Persian. Thus, armed with an amalgamated New Persian, skilled Muslim warriors headed for India. And it was their language that became the language of administration in India, eventually developing an exquisite literary tradition. For after the Muslim conquerors established the Delhi Sultanate in India at the turn of the thirteenth century, Persian remained the official language of India until 1832. Subsequently, in the course of these six centuries, a large amount of Persian, and through it Arabic and Turkic words, found their way into Hindi and other New Indo-Aryan languages.

During the second half of Muslim rule, in the era of the Mughals, European powers struggling for naval supremacy reached India. This Age of Discovery, along with its ensuing Age of Commerce, brought several European nations to India, and with them came exposure of the New Indo-Aryan subgroup to several European languages. The first to arrive was Vasco da Gama in 1498, on the Malabar Coast of India in Calicut. His presence soon brought to the region an increase in Portuguese traders who were an important economical imperium in India until about 1530. And although these Iberians never actually ruled India, they did possess some factories, like in Goa, up until the mid-twentieth century, thus influencing South Asian culture and the Hindi language.

A second European nation to make its mark on Indian bureaucracy, culture, and society was England, with its British Raj. As early as 1600, the English Crown indirectly engaged in trade with India, supplying royal charters to the East India Company. However, it did not officially rule India until 1858, ultimately controlling the territory up to 1947. Throughout this century of formal colonialism, English was the medium for administration, communication, and education,[6] thereby affecting the evolution of Hindi. In this period, knowledge of English became crucial for anybody who wanted to partake in or interact with

6. See Macaulay's minutes from 1835 in which he explains why English should be the language for education and communication in India. "Macaulay," accessed on October 30, 2015, http://www.columbia.edu/itc/mealac/pritchett/00generallinks/macaulay/txt_minute_education_1835.html.

the British government, and as such English became a linguistic bridge, uniting speakers of the many mutually unintelligible languages of India. Hence, it remained prestigious long after India's Independence. To this day, many people in all kinds of situations code-switch and code-mix between Hindi and English, especially in urban areas and in foreign diaspora communities. Apart from this practice, Hindi speakers of the twenty-first century also freely interpolate English words into Hindi sentences, both oral and written. This hybrid variety is sometimes referred to as "Hinglish," in which English nouns and adjectives feature prominently in sentences that retain Hindi verbs, grammar, and syntax. Hinglish can often be heard on TV, in commercial ads, in Bollywood films, on social media, and in communications among urban youth. And alongside it is the heightened use of the Roman script in written applications, often referred to as Romanagari.[7]

I.2. TWO SISTER LANGUAGES

Hindi, though closely related to multiple Northern New Indo-Aryan languages, shares its closest but most complicated relationship with Urdu. Hindi sometimes has been erroneously labeled "the language of the Hindus," while Urdu at times has been ignorantly tagged as "the language of the Muslims." However, many people claim that the two languages are identical, apart from the script in which they are written. The identification of the language written in Devanagari as Hindi and the language written in the Perso-Arabic Nastaliq script as Urdu is only a very recent, and inaccurate, phenomenon. Until around the turn of the twentieth century, "Hindi," "Urdu," and "Hindustani" were used interchangeably, and when referring to the written languages, the terms could refer to a language written in either script. Thus, today some South Asians still use these names as synonyms, with Hindi and Urdu referred to as "Hindi-Urdu."

While the reasons for the identification of Hindi as Hindu and Urdu as Muslim are manifold, the 1947 Partition of India that created the modern nation-states of India and Pakistan clearly changed the

7. "Romanagari," accessed on November 2, 2015, https://en.wikipedia.org/wiki/Romanagari.

dynamics between Hindu and Muslim communities. As a consequence, the relationship between Hindi and Urdu was also transformed. Both languages, subsequently, were selected as official languages of their respective newly formed nations in the aftermath of Independence. India unambiguously stated in its Constitution that the official language was Hindi, meaning Hindi in Devanagari script.[8] Pakistan, in contrast, selected Urdu as its official language, with no details about the script,[9] although it was understood to mean Urdu in the modified Perso-Arabic Nastaliq script. Thus, as the new nations came to be formed from religion, so too were their "national languages" increasingly identified with their corresponding religious communities.[10] The link between the scripts and cultural heritages (Perso-Arabic script and Islam on the one hand, and Devanagari and Hinduism on the other hand) was made more evident in the written word than it had ever been in the spoken language.

Since Independence, numerous books and articles have been written addressing the question whether Hindi and Urdu are one or two languages. Many linguists today consider Hindi and Urdu as two separate New Indo-Aryan languages, even though they share up to 82 percent of their everyday lexicon.[11] Resources such as *Ethnologue* list Hindi and Urdu separately, although under Hindi, Urdu is listed as one of the four dialects of Hindi. This web publication further states that Hindi is the "language of India,"[12] with an additional comment that "Hindi, Hindustani, and Urdu could be considered co-dialects, but have important sociolinguistic differences." Urdu, in comparison, is described by *Ethnologue* as "intelligible with Hindi, but formal vocabulary borrowed from Arabic and Persian." As well, Urdu is listed

8. "Constitution of India," accessed on October 22, 2015, http://indiankanoon.org/doc/379861/.
9. "Constitution of Pakistan," article 251, accessed on November 2, 2015, http://www.pakistani.org/pakistan/constitution/part12.ch4.html.
10. "National languages" is here put in quotation marks, because there is ample controversy over the status as national language for Urdu in Pakistan, and for Hindi in India.
11. Prasad and Virk, *Hindi and Urdu*, 10, accessed on November 30, 2015, http://www.aclweb.org/anthology/W12-5001.
12. "Ethnologue: Hindi," accessed on November 5, 2015, https://www.ethnologue.com/language/hin.

as the "language of Pakistan,"[13] and in the comments section it reads "Muslim." Unfortunately, such a political approach to the status of and relationship between both languages does not do justice to the actual linguistic similarities and numerous elements shared by the two languages. The history of both languages is intertwined and, in spoken form, both languages can be virtually the same. It is obvious from examples like this one that, in modern times, the script has increasingly become a marker of the languages. Grammatically speaking, only some minor differences arise between Hindi and Urdu. For many everyday purposes, however, the languages remain near identical in their spoken form. For official use, Hindi can draw more heavily on vocabulary with a Sanskrit origin, while Urdu can be manipulated to use a higher percentage of words with a Perso-Arabic origin. The governments of India and Pakistan often push this potential divergence to its extreme, making the two languages sound very different. However, it must be noted that this is merely a lexical variation, and the grammar between both languages remains shared. Thus, students who study Hindi grammar will have knowledge of Urdu grammar as well. The most clear addition to complete a student's grammatical knowledge of Urdu, when compared with Hindi, is the *ezafe* construction in Urdu, which has rather limited use in everyday Urdu.[14]

It has become increasingly complicated to give an estimate of the number of Hindi speakers, because of the change in identification of Hindi and Urdu as one versus two languages. It is striking that in 2013, *Ethnologue* listed the number of Hindi and Urdu speakers together to represent a first-language-speaker community of close to 500 million speakers,[15] while in 2015, that number was recorded at about 320 million.[16] This is not due to a drop in the actual number of speakers, but due to the changing definitions of the languages, along with a transition in counting first-language speakers versus simply

13. "Ethnologue: Urdu," accessed on November 5, 2015, https://www.ethnologue.com/language/urd.
14. For additional information on the (current) use of *ezafe* in Hindi and Urdu, see Everaert, *Tracing the Boundaries*, 121–132.
15. "Ethnologue," accessed on September 18, 2013, http://www.ethnologue.com/.
16. See footnotes 12 and 13.

"speakers." When looking at the census of India of 2001, the most recent available census for data on language, the number of Hindi speakers in India is listed as 422 million. The government projected Hindi as the predominant language of 41 percent of the population, but spoken by almost 54 percent.[17] Urdu is not included in the community of Hindi speakers, and it adds 51 million speakers in India alone.[18] The impact of the definitions of Hindi and Urdu causes discrepancies in the estimate of speakers. In Pakistan, only 8 percent of Pakistan's 200 million people indicate that Urdu is their first language. However, it is the lingua franca, and the majority of Pakistani people can speak and understand Urdu.

While the bulk of Hindi and Urdu speakers reside in India and Pakistan, important minority communities of Hindi and Urdu speakers can be found all over the world, in places such as the United Kingdom, the United States, South Africa, Uganda, Zanzibar, the United Arab Emirates, Oman, Bahrain, Trinidad, the Fiji Islands, and Singapore. It is safe to say that depending on how one defines Hindi and Urdu, and depending on whether one counts L1 and/or L2 speakers of Hindi and Urdu, between 5 and 10 percent of the world's population can be referred to as speakers of Hindi and/or Urdu. Some sources even go as far as stating that "Combined, the languages of Hindi and Urdu are spoken by almost a billion people across Pakistan and India."[19]

In the end, though, whichever way one counts, studying Hindi, Urdu, or Hindi-Urdu and its grammar will open the door to communication with hundreds of millions of people, while introducing many millions of pages of rich literature that have been produced over many decades, if not centuries.

---

17. "Census of India," accessed on November 10, 2015, http://www.censusindia.gov.in/Ad_Campaign/press/DataHighlghts.pdf.
18. "Census of India," accessed on November 10, 2015, http://www.censusindia.gov.in/%28S%282scoev45b4mhlg45mz5jq345%29%29/Census_Data_2001/Census_Data_Online/Language/Statement1.aspx.
19. "CLS Hindi," accessed on November 15, 2015, http://www.clscholarship.org/languages/hindi.

PART II

The Hindi Alphabet

I. THE ALPHABET (वर्णमाला VARṆAMĀLĀ)

The Hindi alphabet is phonemic and consists of forty-four letters, eleven of which are vowels. The Devanagari script does not have capital letters at the beginning of sentences or names.

The alphabet was organized by Sanskrit grammarian Panini in such a way that it starts with the vowels. The consonants follow, organized by place and mode of pronunciation. Reading the following five tables horizontally from left to right, offers the correct alphabetical order as found in Hindi dictionaries.

I.1. THE VOWELS (स्वर SVAR)

Orthographically, the first eleven letters of the Hindi alphabet, the vowels, are the most complex. The short vowel 'a' is pronounced after every consonant, but is not represented in the script by a separate letter, except at the beginning of a word, or following another vowel in the middle of a word, e.g., अगर (agar) 'if', सुअर (suar) 'pig'. In the latter case, the second vowel being written in its initial, independent form represents a glottal stop between two vowels.

Contrary to the consonants, the vowels are written in two ways: they have an independent, initial, or syllabic form, sometimes called अक्षर (akṣar) when they appear at the beginning of a word, or following another vowel, and they have an intra-syllabic, dependent, or मात्रा (mātrā) form, when following a consonant.

Table 1. The vowels

VOWEL			E.G., IN COMBINATION WITH THE CONSONANT K			
	INITIAL, INDEPENDENT FORM	मात्रा (MĀTRĀ) FOLLOWING A CONSONANT, DEPENDENT FORM	INITIAL		MĀTRĀ FOLLOWING K	
a	अ		ak	अक	ka	क
ā	आ	ा	āk	आक	kā	का
i	इ	ि	ik	इक	ki	कि
ī	ई	ी	īk	ईक	kī	की
u	उ	ु	uk	उक	ku	कु
ū	ऊ	ू	ūk	ऊक	kū	कू
ṛ	ऋ	ृ	ṛk	ऋक	kṛ	कृ
e	ए	े	ek	एक	ke	के
ai	ऐ	ै	aik	ऐक	kai	कै
o	ओ	ो	ok	ओक	ko	को
au	औ	ौ	auk	औक	kau	कौ

Table 2. Guide to the pronunciation of the vowels

VOWEL			
	INITIAL	MĀTRĀ FOLLOWING	PRONOUNCE AS THE VOWEL IN BOLD IN FOLLOWING ENGLISH WORD
a	अ		**a**broad, **a**gain
ā	आ	ा	Ut**a**h, f**a**ther
i	इ	ि	s**i**ngle, s**i**p
ī	ई	ी	d**ee**r, m**ea**n
u	उ	ु	l**oo**k, c**oo**k
ū	ऊ	ू	d**oo**m, r**oo**m
ṛ	ऋ	ृ	**ri**ddle, b**ri**ttle
e	ए	े	sh**a**ke, l**a**ke
ai	ऐ	ै	d**ai**ry, h**ai**r
o	ओ	ो	r**o**pe, h**o**pe
au	औ	ौ	m**ou**ntain, f**ou**nd

I.2. THE CONSONANTS (व्यंजन VYAÑJAN)

The majority of the letters representing consonants in the Devanagari alphabet is built around the vertical stroke: ा. This vertical stroke symbolizes the short vowel 'a' that is pronounced after every consonant, but is not represented in the script by a separate letter.

The consonants are organized according to place of articulation, starting at the back of the oral cavity, and moving forward toward the front of the mouth. One can discern five groups of sounds: velar/ guttural (pronounced on the soft palate, at the back of the mouth), palatal (pronounced with the tongue raised to the hard palate), cerebral (pronounced with the tip of the tongue on the alveolar ridge), dental (pronounced with the tip of the tongue against the teeth), and labial (pronounced on the lips). By paying attention to the place of articulation, the correct pronunciation of unfamiliar sounds can be ameliorated.

I.2.1. THE OCCLUSIVES OR PLOSIVES (स्पर्श SPARŚ) AND NASAL SOUNDS (अनुनासिक ANUNĀSIK)

There is a difference between place of articulation and mode of articulation. The first group of consonants share the way in which they are articulated: they are all plosives or occlusives. A plosive or occlusive is a letter (consonants only) that is characterized by an explosion of sound, created by releasing a blockage of the airflow. As a consequence, and contrary to nasal or fricative sounds (see below), plosive sounds cannot be lengthened. Within this category, they are organized according to place of articulation. Every group of occlusive consonants is supplemented by a corresponding nasal sound. The following tables should be read left to right, over the full length of the table, in order to read them in alphabetical order.

Table 3. The occlusives or plosives and nasal sounds

	OCCLUSIVES				
	VOICELESS		VOICED[1]		NASAL
	UNASPIRATED	ASPIRATED[2]	UNASPIRATED	ASPIRATED	VOICED
Velar or guttural	ka क	kha ख	ga ग	gha घ	ṅa ङ
Palatal	ca च	cha छ	ja ज	jha झ	ña ञ
Cerebral	ṭa ट	ṭha ठ	ḍa ड	ḍha ढ	ṇa ण
Dental	ta त	tha थ	da द	dha ध	na न
Labial	pa प	pha फ	ba ब	bha भ	ma म

[1] For voiceless consonants, one does not use one's vocal cords when pronouncing the sound. The voiced counterpart means that the sound is made by putting the tongue on the same spot as for the voiceless counterpart, but the vocal cords are used while doing so. Physically, one can tell the difference between a voiced and voiceless sound by placing the hand on the throat when pronouncing a consonant (do not pronounce any vowel following it, as all vowels are voiced). If the throat vibrates while pronouncing a consonant, it is voiced. If there is no vibration, the consonant is voiceless. Hence, if the hand is placed on the throat while saying 'k' (without an 'a' following), no vibration will be felt. However, if one pronounces a 'g' (as in 'garden') without an 'a' following, the throat will vibrate.

[2] Aspirated means that one blows or produces a burst of air while pronouncing the correlating unaspirated consonant. Example: for 'k' vs. 'kh': there is no burst of air when saying 'k'. But when one pronounces 'kh', the sound is made in the same place and way as 'k', but if the hand is placed in front of the mouth, one will feel a pronounced blow of air on the hand while saying 'kh', but much less so when saying 'k'.

In order to pronounce all the above consonants, the tongue has to be moved only five times, from the back to the front of the mouth.

Table 4. Guide to the pronunciation of the occlusives and nasals

CONSONANT		PRONOUNCE AS THE CONSONANT IN BOLD IN FOLLOWING ENGLISH WORD
ka	क	**k**ing, **c**obra
kha*[1]	ख	**ch**aos, al**ch**emy
ga	ग	lu**gg**age, **g**obble
gha*	घ	**gh**oul, au**g**ury, do**gh**ouse
ṅa	ङ	a**n**kle, ba**n**gle
ca	च	**ch**allenge, **ch**in
cha*	छ	**ch**ocolate, **ch**amber
ja	ज	**j**ungle, **j**olly
jha*	झ	no equivalent; as in 'jungle' but exhale while pronouncing
ña	ञ	Pu**n**jab, beni**gn**
ṭa*	ट	(not exact) loi**t**er, rec**t**ify
ṭha*	ठ	no equivalent; as in 'loiter' but exhale while pronouncing
ḍa*	ड	(not exact) roun**d**about
ḍha*	ढ	no equivalent; as in 'roundabout' but exhale while pronouncing
ṇa*	ण	(not exact) rou**n**dabout
ta	त	**t**ooth, **t**able
tha	थ	no equivalent; as in 'tooth' but exhale while pronouncing
da	द	**d**octor, **d**onkey
dha*	ध	no equivalent; as in 'doctor' but exhale while pronouncing
na	न	**n**ou**n**, **n**ight
pa	प	**p**a**p**er, **p**ass**p**ort
pha*	फ	no equivalent; as in 'paper' but exhale while pronouncing
ba	ब	lim**b**er, **b**o**b**cat
bha*	भ	no equivalent; as in 'limber' but exhale while pronouncing
ma	म	**m**oose, **m**elon

[1] No exact example for the pronounciation can be given for retroflex or cerebral sounds, nor for aspirated consonants, as they do not really exist in English. For all letters followed by an asterisk, an example in English has been given that will sound as close as possible. To correctly pronounce cerebral letters, place the tip of the tongue to the alveolar ridge instead of the back of the teeth when pronouncing their dental equivalent.

I.2.2. THE LIQUIDS OR SEMI-VOCALS (स्वर-सदृश SVAR-SADṚŚ)

Table 5. The liquids or semi-vocals

	VOICELESS		VOICED	
	UNASPIRATED	ASPIRATED	UNASPIRATED	ASPIRATED
Velar or guttural				
Palatal			ya य	
Cerebral			ra र	
Dental			la ल	
Labio-dental			va व	

Table 6. Guide to the pronunciation of the liquids

CONSONANT		PRONOUNCE AS THE CONSONANT IN BOLD IN FOLLOWING ENGLISH WORD
ya	य	**y**esterda**y**, **y**oung
ra	र	Spanish '**r**eal', 'a**rr**iba'
la	ल	**l**ong, **l**abel
va	व	**w**inter, **v**o**w**el (actually in between v and w)

I.2.3. THE FRICATIVES[1] (सघर्षी SANGHARṢĪ)

Table 7. The fricatives

	VOICELESS		VOICED	
	UNASPIRATED	ASPIRATED	UNASPIRATED	ASPIRATED
Velar or guttural				
Palatal	śa श			
Cerebral	ṣa[1] ष			
Dental	sa स			
Labial				

[1] In modern Hindi, the palatal ś श and cerebral ṣ ष are both pronounced palatally.

Table 8. Guide to the pronunciation of the fricatives

CONSONANT		PRONOUNCE AS THE CONSONANT IN BOLD IN FOLLOWING ENGLISH WORD
śa	श	**sh**awl, **sh**ower
ṣa	ष	**sh**awl, **sh**ower
sa	स	**s**ong, **s**i**s**ter

I.2.4. THE ASPIRATES (ह-ध्वनि HA-DHVANI)

Table 9. The aspirates

VOICELESS		VOICED	
UNASPIRATED	ASPIRATED	UNASPIRATED	ASPIRATED
			ha ह

1. One can hear the word 'friction' in the term 'fricative'. A fricative is a consonant that is pronounced by forcing air through a narrow opening in the mouth, e.g., between lip and teeth, or tongue and teeth, which causes friction, producing a sound.

Table 10. Guide to the pronunciation of the aspirates

CONSONANT		PRONOUNCE AS THE CONSONANT IN BOLD IN FOLLOWING ENGLISH WORD
ha	ह	**h**and, **h**ungry

I.2.5. VARIANTS BASED ON THE BASIC LETTERS

A few variants of basic consonants exist that differ from those basic letters only by the addition of a diacritic dot underneath the letter. The addition of these letters were mainly necessary to be able to represent introduced sounds that are found in words with Persian, Arabic, and Turkic etymology, as well as for sounds used when writing words with sounds alien to Sanskrit and Prakrits, but present in words with Portuguese and English origin.

These variants are not listed separately in dictionaries. They are listed under the basic letters. In colloquial Hindi, many variants are pronounced as if the diacritic dot were not there, hence making no distinction between the basic letter and the variant: e.g., प्याज pyāj for pyāz 'onion'; खिडकी khiḍkī for khiṛkī 'window'. See the following table.

Table 11. Variants based on the basic letters

BASIC LETTER		VARIANT	
Variant of Persian or Arabic origin			
ka	क	qa	क़
kha	ख	ḵẖa	ख़
ga	ग	g̱a	ग़
ja	ज	za	ज़
pha	फ	fa	फ़
Variant of non-Persian or Arabic origin			
ḍa	ड	ṛa	ड़
ḍha	ढ	ṛha	ढ़

Table 12. Guide to the pronunciation of the variants

CONSONANT		PRONOUNCE AS THE CONSONANT IN BOLD IN FOLLOWING ENGLISH WORD
qa	क़	(not exact) **q**uestion, li**q**uor
k͟ha	ख़	Scottish 'lo**ch**'
g̱a*	ग़	closer to the 'French r'
za	ज़	**z**ebra, **z**oo
fa	फ़	**f**estival, li**f**t
ṛa*	ड़	(not exact) as in 'ba**r**be**r**'
ṛha*	ढ़	no equivalent; as in 'ba**r**be**r**' but exhale while pronouncing

I.3. THE PRONUNCIATION (उच्चारण UCCĀRAṆ) OF THE INHERENT SHORT VOWEL A TO THE SYLLABIC CHARACTER[2]

As Devanagari is an abugida or alphasyllabary alphabet, in which consonant-vowel sequences are written as one unit, consonants are normally pronounced with the inherent short vowel 'a' included. The short 'a' is pronounced when the word only contains two consonants, e.g., 'when?' कब (kab), 'house' घर (ghar). However:

1. The 'a' is not pronounced after the final consonant of a word, e.g., the word for 'day' is दिन (din, not dina). The word न (na) 'not' as well as words ending in ह (ha) are the exceptions. In the latter case, a sort of echo arises, e.g., in case of the numbers like eleven: ग्यारह (gyāraha), etc. The same is true for the words ending in a ligature, e.g., उग्र (ugra) 'anger', अभिज्ञ (abhijña/abhigya) 'well informed'.

2. I use the term 'syllabic character' here for Hindi in Devanagari script. One cannot use the word 'syllable', as the short inherent 'a' is not pronounced consistently in Hindi, as was the case in Sanskrit. As a result, loan words from Sanskrit often have a syllable less in Hindi than they have in Sanskrit, despite it being the same word, written in the same way. E.g., कर्म (karma) is in Hindi monosyllabic (karm), while it is disyllabic in Sanskrit (kar-ma). Moreover, one cannot simply use the word 'letter' or 'sign', as a ligature of two or more consonants are treated as a single letter or sign. Vowels are indeed written separately, but often form an unbreakable cluster with a consonant, so one cannot use the word 'letter'. Often, two 'letters' make one whole.

One notices that it is near impossible to pronounce those words without pronouncing the final 'a'.[3]

2. When a word consists of three consonants, all inherent short 'a's', except for the final one, are pronounced, e.g.: रहन (rahan) 'lifestyle', भवन (bhavan) 'abode', तरफ़ (taraf) 'side'. However, there are exceptions to this rule, e.g., ज़हर (zahr) 'poison'.
3. The 'a' is not pronounced between two consecutive consonants, when a virām is written, or a ligature (संयुक्ताक्षर samyuktākṣar) is used. (See I.4.) E.g.: बच्चा (baccā) 'child', विद्यार्थी (vidyārthī) 'student'.[4]
4. Sometimes, the inherent short 'a' is not (or hardly) pronounced, without it being evident from the orthography. When a word consists of three or more syllabic characters, and the word ends in a vowel that is not the short 'a' (i.e., -ā, -i, -ī, -u, -ū, -e, -ai, -o, -au), or the word contains more than three consonants, the short 'a' of the second syllabic character will not be pronounced, e.g., करना (kar-nā) 'to do', चकमा (cak-mā) 'deception', अपनी (ap-nī) 'one's own' (f.), लड़कों (laṛ-koṃ) 'boys' (obl.pl.), पहचान (pah-cān) 'recognition'.

Many verbs have inherent short 'a's that are not pronounced without it being evident from the orthography. Basically, the root of verbs follows the above rules, but not the infinitive or conjugated form. The root behaves as if it is an independent word, and follows the above formulated rules, depending on whether or not the root ends in a consonant or vowel, and how many syllabic characters there are in the root. The ending indicating the tense of the verb is simply added, after pronouncing the root as an independent word. So, if the root with up to three consonants ends in a consonant, all but the final short 'a's of the root are pronounced. However, when the last letter of the root is a vowel, or contains over three consonants, the inherent short 'a' of the second syllabic character of the root will not be pronounced.

3. Note that in colloquial speech, words ending in 'h' might be pronounced as if they end in 'a', or even 'ā', and the 'h' sound might be dropped altogether.
4. For the ending of the word 'student', see ligatures with the consonant 'r' (infra).

Examples:

'to recognize' पहचानना (pahcān-nā)
'to appear' निकलना (nikal-nā)

'to change' बदलना (badal-nā)	BUT	'to cause to change' बदलाना (badlā-nā)
'to shine' चमकना (camak-nā)	BUT	'causing to shine' चमकाते (camkā-te)
'to catch' पकड़ना (pakaṛ-nā)	BUT	'having caused to be caught' पकड़ाकर (pakṛā-kar)
'to crackle' कड़कना (kaṛak-nā)	BUT	'caused to crackle' कड़कड़ाया (kaṛkaṛā-yā)

At first sight, compound words too can seem exceptions to the rules. However, these words follow the above formulated rules when the different components of compound words are seen as separate words. As a consequence, the final -a of the different components will never be pronounced, e.g., in the word हमसफ़र (ham-safar) 'companion', the inherent 'a' after the letter म (ma) is not pronounced. This can be explained because the word is a compound of co-, हम (ham) 'fellow', + सफ़र (safar) 'travel, journey'; किताबघर (kitāb-ghar) 'bookshop' = किताब (kitāb) 'book' + घर (ghar) 'house'; हिमनद (him-nad) 'glacier' = हिम (him) 'ice, snow' + नद (nad) 'river'.

When one is not aware of the etymology of a word, and does not recognize a word as a compound word, it might be hard to predict which short 'a' will be silent. Recognizing prefixes and suffixes can help accurately pronounce compound words, as compound words do not only consist of a combination of nouns, but also of nouns with prefixes or suffixes. (See IX.1. and IX.2. for a list of common prefixes and suffixes.)

I.4. THE LIGATURES (संयुक्ताक्षर SAṂYUKTĀKṢAR)

I.4.1. LIGATURES OF TWO OR MORE CONSONANTS

In some cases, when the short 'a' of a consonant is not pronounced, that consonant is not written as a full letter, but fuses with the following consonant. The fusion of two or more consonants is called a ligature. Instead of a ligature, it is also possible to write a virām (्) underneath the half consonant, i.e., the consonant of which the inherent short 'a' should not be pronounced. E.g., instead of the ligature ट्ट, one can also write ट्‌ट (ṭṭa).

With respect to the script, it is important to know that a ligature becomes one unbreakable whole, and vowels following the cluster cannot break up the union of the ligature in script. This is especially important when a ligature is followed by the short vowel 'i', e.g., मुश्किल (muśkil) 'difficult': the ligature श्क (śk, combination of श (ś) and क (k)) is acting as one letter, and the short vowel 'i' is written before the ligature (श्कि śki), not between the two fused consonants.

Traditionally, the three ligatures क्ष (kṣa), त्र (tra), and ज्ञ (gya/jña)[5] are considered to be the last three letters of the Hindi alphabet, following the ह ha. However, they are not listed separately in dictionaries and can be found under क (k), त (t), and ज (j), respectively.

I.4.2. THE र (RA) IN A LIGATURE

Orthographically speaking, the letter र (ra) behaves rather peculiarly when part of a ligature.

1. c + र (ra)

When the र (ra) is the second consonant of a ligature of two consonants, it is written as a small diagonal stroke from the right top to the left bottom (mirroring the virām) e.g., pra प्र, kra क्र, bra ब्र, or gra ग्र. Underneath the letters ट ṭa, ठ ṭha, ḍa ड, and ढ ḍha, the 'r' is written as ‸: ट्र ṭra, ठ्र ṭhra, ड्र ḍra, and ḍhra ढ्र.

2. र (ra) + c(c)

When the र (ra) is the first consonant of a ligature, it is written as र्‍ (रेफ (reph)), on top of the last consonant of the ligature, e.g., rk in पॉर्क 'park', rdr in आर्द्रता (ārdratā) 'humidity', rtt in the name of the Hindu month कार्त्तिक (kārttik). However, when the consonant cluster is

5. Even though the modern pronunciation has shifted to 'gy', etymologically, this ligature is the combination of 'ज' (j) and 'ञ' (ñ), and consequently, this ligature can only be found under 'ज' (j) in a dictionary, and not under 'ग' (g).

followed by a long vowel 'ā' of 'ī', the reph is written on top of this long vowel instead of on top of the last consonant, e.g., वर्षा (varṣā) 'rain', कुर्सी (kursī) 'chair'.

I.4.3. THE ANUSVĀR (अनुस्वार)

There are five nasals in the Devanagari alphabet.

ṅa ङ
ña ञ
ṇa ण
na न
ma म

When nasals occur as the first consonant in a ligature, these five half nasals can be written as ˙ (called anusvār). Because a nasal in a ligature can only be followed by a consonant that has the same place of articulation, the anusvār can only stand for one letter: a dental nasal written as anusvār is always followed by a dental consonant, a cerebral nasal by a cerebral consonant, etc. As a result, one can write 'Punjab' as पंजाब or पञ्जाब (pañjāb), 'cold' as ठंडा or ठण्डा (ṭhaṇḍā), 'Hindi' as हिंदी or हिन्दी (hindī), 'long' as लंबा or लम्बा (lambā). As the anusvār is a half a letter, and not a nasalizing sound, that occurs only as the first letter of a ligature, it is obvious that a word can never end in an anusvār. (See the following section for the difference between a nasal letter and nasalization.)

I.5. THE NASALIZATION OR ANUNĀSIK (अनुनासिक)

Apart from the vowel ऋ (ṛ), every vowel can be nasalized. A nasalization is represented by the candrabindu ('the moon and the drop' or 'the drop in the moon'), written as ँ. In transliteration, this sign is often written as 'ṃ' or 'ṁ', or by placing the tilde ~ over the vowel that is nasalized, e.g., अँ could be transliterated as 'aṃ', 'aṁ', or 'ã'.

Note: an anusvār is a nasal letter in a ligature; the dot thus represents half a letter. The anunāsik is a nasalization, not a letter. Often, editors are rather sloppy and write both the anusvār and anunāsik as a dot ('drop' ˙), without the 'moon' ˘. As a result, an anusvār is written, while it should be an anunāsik. In reality, those two signs are not one and the same.

However, an anusvār is consistently written for an anunāsik when a word ends in a nasalized vowel (-ī, -e, -ai, -o, or -au). This is simply due to typographical reasons. As a consequence, all nouns in the oblique plural case (ending in -oṃ), all female nouns with plural ending -eṃ, f. pl. participles (ending in -īṃ), and the verb 'to be' in 3 pl. always use anunāsik for the anusvār. A few examples: 'women' औरतें 'never' औरतेँ (auratem̥); 'are' हैं 'never' हैँ (haiṃ); 'sisters' (obl.) बहनों 'never' बहनोँ (bahanoṃ).

The candra or the 'moon' ˘ is written on top of the long vowel ा (ā) to represent vowels in English words that are in between the Hindi sound 'ā' (open vowel) and 'o' (close-mid vowel o), e.g., 'George' जॉर्ज, 'coffee' कॉफ़ी.

I.6. THE VISARGA (विसर्ग)

In some tatsama Sanskrit words,[6] one comes across the visarga. This is a voiceless aspiration. The sign looks like a colon ः, e.g., दुःख (duḥkh) 'grief'; छः (chaḥ) 'six'. In modern texts, the visarga is less and less used, either simply dropped or replaced by the letter ह (h), e.g., दुख (dukh) 'grief'; छह (chah, colloquially often pronounced as 'che') 'six'.

I.7. PUNCTUATION MARKS (विराम-चिह्न VIRĀM-CIHN)

Traditionally, Hindi, just like Sanskrit, did not use punctuation marks, except for pūrṇ virām, written as a vertical stroke ।. This mark serves the function of a full stop at the end of a sentence.

Presently, all Western punctuation marks (comma, colon, semicolon, etc.) are used increasingly, allbeit not systematically. However, even when Western punctuation is used in a text, the full stop is not used, and pūrṇ virām indicates the end of a sentence instead. When initials and abbreviations are used, the dots between the letters are written as °, e.g., D. C. Paṭel is written as डी ° सी ° पटेल (ḍī. sī. paṭel).

The question mark is often replaced by a simple pūrṇ virām.

6. Tatsama words are loan words that have retained their Sanskrit form in Hindi. Tadbhava words are nouns that did not retain their Sanskrit form, but underwent phonological changes in the different Prakrits. Apart from tatsama and tadbhava words, there are also deśī or desi words, i.e., "native" words that do not necessarily have a Sanskritic etymology.

This is especially the case for rhetorical questions or inner, reflective thoughts, e.g., in the *Pañcatantra* story चूहे और हाथी (cūhe aur hāthī 'The mice and elephants': अब चूहे उन हाथियों को कैसे रोकें जिससे वे उन्हें हानि न पहुँचा सकें। (ab cūhe un hāthiyoṃ ko kaise rokeṃ jisse ve unheṃ hāni na pahuṃcā sakeṃ). 'Now how could the mice stop the elephants so that they would not be able to cause them harm.' The interrogative participle कैसे would ordinarily require a question mark, but as this is a reflective thought on the mice's part, the question mark is absent, replaced by a pūrṇ virām.

PART III

Basic Hindi Grammar

I. CASES (कारक KĀRAK) VERSUS USAGE OF POSTPOSITIONS (परसर्ग PARSARG)

I.1. INTRODUCTION

A grammatical case is an altered or inflected form of a noun, adjective, or pronoun that gives an indication of the function of the word or word group in the sentence. In Hindi, contrary to Sanskrit, Latin, German, or other languages that still employ cases, the function of a word or word group is generally no longer indicated by the usage of a specific case.[1] Postpositions have taken over the function of most cases. Because the different word groups no longer have their own distinct declension to show their function in the sentence, one could say that postpositions fulfill the function of all cases, except for the nominative case, which is used for subjects and predicates, and is constructed without a postposition (see infra).

Technically, there are three cases left in Hindi: the vocative case, the nominative case, and the oblique case. The vocative case is used scarcely. Simplified, one could state that in Hindi, a word or word group is put in either the nominative or the not-nominative case, i.e., the oblique case (विकारी कारक vikārī kārak). Whenever a postposition is used, all the words of the word group that ends with the postposition are put into the oblique case.

I.2. THE DIFFERENT CASES

I.2.1. THE VOCATIVE CASE (संबोधन कारक SAMBODHAN KĀRAK)

The vocative case is used when addressing somebody. However, in Hindi, the vocative case is most frequently applied when kinship terms are used to address somebody. This form is still commonly used in public speeches to address the crowds (भाइयो (bhāiyo) 'brethren'). A famous example can be heard in Mohammad Rafi's song, written following the assassination of Gandhi in 1948, सुनो सुनो ऐ दुनिया <u>वालो</u> बापू की यह अमर कहानी (suno suno ai duniyā <u>vālo</u> bāpū kī yah amar kahānī): "Listen, listen, <u>o people</u> of the world, to this immortal story of Bāpū"

1. Classical Sanskrit has eight different cases for the declension of nouns, Latin has six, and German has four.

('Father', i.e., Gandhi). When using words like 'sir', 'madam', and 'miss', the vocative case is no longer used.

I.2.2. THE NOMINATIVE CASE (कर्त्ता कारक KARTTĀ KĀRAK)

Both the subject and the predicate in a sentence are always put in the nominative case. A predicate can be defined as fulfilling the function of a direct object in other sentences, but in this case, the main verb is the verb 'to be' (होना honā). When the verb is 'to be', there is a direct link between the subject and the direct object, contrary to sentences that have a main verb other than 'to be'. As a consequence, the direct object is called predicate instead, and subject and predicate agree with each other in gender, number, as well as grammatical case, being the nominative case.

Examples:

Lālū / was / a very clever monkey. (Gulzār)
Subj. Pred. (Nom.)

लालू / बहुत चालाक बंदर / था। (lālū bahut cālāk bandar thā)
Nom. Nom.

My heart / is / so weak. (Varmā)
Subj. Pred. (Nom.)

मेरा हृद्य / इतना निर्बल / है। (merā hṛdya itnā nirbal hai.)
Nom.m sg Nom.m sg

[She] / was / very good, / the poor woman. (Premcand)
Subj. Pred. (Nom.)

बड़ी अच्छी / थी / बेचारी। (baṛī acchī thī becārī.)
Nom.f sg Nom.f sg

Twenty years ago, / I / was / a Hindu woman. (Ugra)
Subj. Pred. (Nom.)

मैं / आज से बीस वर्ष पहले / हिन्दू-ललना / थी। (maiṃ āj se bīs sāl pahle hindū lalnā thī.)
Nom.f sg Nom.f sg

I.2.3. THE OBLIQUE CASE (विकारी कारक VIKĀRĪ KĀRAK)

The oblique case is used whenever the last word of a word group is a postposition, whether implicit (see I.2.3.1.1. and I.2.3.2.) or explicit. All the words within that word group turn into the oblique case. One can differentiate the function of the various word groups according to the postposition instead of the different cases. As Hindi uses postpositions, contrary to prepositions in English, you could say that the oblique case warns the listener that the words one is hearing are not the subject or predicate of the sentence, and hence he or she has to listen to the postposition in order to find out what the function of the word group in oblique will be.

I.2.3.1. OBLIQUE CASE USED WITH POSTPOSITION को (KO)

In Sanskrit, the accusative case is used for time and place indications, as well as direct objects. In Hindi, it is the postposition को (ko) that can be used to indicate which word (group) is a time or place indication, or the direct object in the sentence.

I.2.3.1.1. TIME AND PLACE INDICATIONS

Words or word groups that are indications of time or place can be constructed using the oblique case, with or without the postposition को (ko) as the last word of the constituent. Only in the case of word groups that are an indication of time or space, the postposition को (ko) is often dropped, but the word group remains in the oblique case, even if the postposition is implied and not expressed: [at] that time: उस समय (us samay), [at] their house: उनके घर (unke ghar). The oblique is never retained when को (ko) is dropped to indicate the direct object (see I.2.3.1.2.). In time and place indications, को (ko) can sometimes be replaced with में (meṃ) or पर (par).[2]

It is important to note that the time and place indications seem to be increasingly constructed without expressing the postposition. Some native speakers of Hindi consider the explicit mention of the postposition wrong or colloquial, especially to express direction or movement, or after time indications. However, many standard Hindi and Urdu grammars explicitly list the use of को (ko) in association with place and time.[3] McGregor elaborates: "Note that sometimes place to which

2. In Sanskrit, this is referred to as the accusative case (कर्म कारक karm kārak).
3. Agnihotri, *Essential Hindi*, 143–146; McGregor, *Outline of Hindi*, 53–55; Sandahl, *Hindi Reference*, 29; Schmidt, *Essential Urdu*, 72, 241; Snell, *ko*, accessed on November 8, 2015, http://hindiurduflagship.org/assets/pdf/Hindi_Ko.pdf.

motion occurs is best indicated by a noun in the oblique case without the following postposition. This is so chiefly when the place concerned is a geographical locality denoted by a place-name, or is otherwise felt as a specific destination. But it is rarely wrong to use को *ko* in such locutions, though in certain cases if a postposition is used, में *meṁ*, पर *par* or की ओर *kī* or, की तरफ़ *kī taraf* may be preferred."[4] Schmidt mentions: "**śām** and **rāt** are used in adverbial expressions of time with the postposition **kī**. With **subah**, **kī** is optional, and with **din**, **meṁ** is used."[5]

Examples:

Come / in the evening! (Gulzār)
time

शाम को / आ जाना। (śām ko ā jānā!)
Acc. (Obl.+ को)

I eat daily / at your house /, but not once did I invite you / to my house.
Place Place
(Gulzār)

रोज़ खाता हूँ / तुम्हारे घर पर / और एक बार भी तुम्हें / अपने घर / नहीं बुलाया। (roz khātā
Acc. (Obl. + पर) Acc. (Obl. but को dropped)
hūṃ tumhāre ghar par aur ek bār bhī tumheṃ apne ghar nahīṃ bulāyā.)

At this moment / both were sitting down and eating *pūṛīs* / this evening.
Time Time
(Premcand)

दोनों / इस वक़्त / इस शाम में / बैठे पूड़ियाँ खा रहे थे। (donoṃ is vaqt is śām meṃ baiṭhe
Acc. (Obl., omitted को) Acc. (Obl. + में)
pūṛiyāṃ khā rahe the.)

I.2.3.1.2. DIRECT OBJECTS WITH AND WITHOUT THE POSTPOSITION को (KO)

Modern Hindi distinguishes between two kinds of direct objects: 'animate'[6] and 'inanimate' (objects, most animals). Both of those can occur as definite/specific (e.g., the, those, my) or indefinite/nonspecific

4. McGregor, *Outline of Hindi*, 54.
5. Schmidt, *Essential Urdu*, 241.
6. Mostly, this means people. However, in stories like the *Pañcatantra* stories, in which the animals also talk, animals are often considered people.

word groups (e.g., a(n), tall, beautiful). The usage of the postposition को (ko) is not random. The usage of को (ko) can be summed up in the following table.

Table 13. Direct objects with and without the postposition को (ko)

	ANIMATE D.O.	INANIMATE D.O.
Definite D.O.	Always को (ko)	को (ko) optional
Indefinite D.O.	Never को (ko)	Never को (ko)

को (ko) is always used when the direct object is definite and animate. को (ko) can be used when the direct object is definite and inanimate. For indefinite direct objects, the indefinite accusative case, which is identical to the nominative case, is used. Indefinite animate and inanimate direct objects are never constructed with the postposition को (ko), and hence the oblique case never occurs.

It is important to note that with direct objects, either को (ko) is expressed, and the word group turns into the oblique case, or को (ko) is not expressed, and the direct object remains in the nominative case. Oblique cannot occur without को (ko) being explicitly expressed.

1. Animate objects

Definite animate direct objects are always constructed with को (ko).

Examples:

After seeing / that young man, / Mahātmājī was amazed. (Ugra)
Def. D.O.

महातमाजी / उस युवक को / देखकर आश्चर्य में आ गए। (mahātmājī us yuvak ko dekhkar
Obl. + को (ko)
āścary meṃ ā gae.)

Someone called / him / from somewhere. (Bismillāh)
Def. D.O.

किसी ने / उसे / कहीं से आवाज़ दी। (kisī ne use kahīṃ se āvāz dī.)
Obl. + को (ko)

Will you forgive / me? (Varmā)
Def. D.O.

मुझे / क्षमा करोगी? (mujhe kṣamā karogī?)
Obl. + को (ko)

Ṭinnū congratulated / himself. (Bismillāh)
Def. D.O.

टिन्नू ने / ख़ुद को / शाबासी दी। (ṭinnū ne khud ko śābāsī dī.)
Obl. + को (ko)

I had never in my life seen / a more base and selfish crocodile / than Nathnī (f.). (Gulzār)
Indef. D.O.

मैंने अपनी ज़िन्दगी में नथनी से / ज़्यादा कमीनी और खुदग़र्ज़ मगरमछ / नहीं देखी। (maiṃ apnī zindagī meṃ nathnī se zyāda kamīnī aur khudgarz magarmach nahīṃ dekhī.)
Nom. without को (ko)

2. Inanimate objects

Definite inanimate direct objects can be constructed with or without को (ko).

Examples:

I saw / all the things / in your room. (Varmā)
Def. D.O.

मैंने तुम्हारे कमरे की / सब चीज़ों को / देखा। (maiṃne tumhāre kamre kī sab cīzoṃ ko dekhā.)
Obl. + को (ko)

May I ask you / one thing? (Varmā)
Indef. D.O.

एक बात / पूछूँ? (ek bāt pūchūṃ?)
Nom. without को (ko)

I saw / my face / in the mirror. (Varmā)
Indef. D.O.

आईना में मैंने / अपना मुख / देखा। (āīnā meṃ maiṃne apnā mukh dekhā.)
Nom. without को (ko)

Remark: An inanimate object that is constructed with को (ko) is more definite than one constructed without को (ko). It is mostly used when referring to a very specific object or an object that has been discussed before.

Examples:

To wash / their sin / away, they bathe in the Ganges. (Premcand)
Def. D.O.

अपने पाप को / धोने के लिए गंगा में नहाते हैं। (apne pāp ko dhone ke lie gaṃgā meṃ
Nom. + को (ko)
nahāte haiṃ.)

I consider / the words of my mother / more holy than the verses of the
Def. D.O.
Qur'ān. (Ugra)

मैं / अपनी माँ की बातों को / क़ुरान शरीफ़ की आयतों से अधिक पवित्र मानता हूँ। (maiṃ apnī māṃ kī bātoṃ ko qurān śarīf kī āyatoṃ se adhik pavitr māntā hūṃ.)
Obl. + को (ko)

I.2.3.2. OBLIQUE CASE USED AS A MARKER OF AN INSTRUMENT, AGENT OR (LACK OF) COMPANION, REASON OR CIRCUMSTANCE OF AN ACTION, IN COMBINATION WITH POSTPOSITIONS LIKE से (SE), के साथ (KE SĀTH), के बिना (KE BINĀ), के द्वारा (KE DVĀRĀ)

Word groups providing information about the instrument through which something happens or is done, or the circumstances in which something happens, are put into the oblique, followed by postpositions like से (se) 'with, through, out of'; के साथ (ke sāth) '(together) with'; के बिना (ke binā) 'without'; के द्वारा (ke dvārā) 'by means or agency of'. In Sanskrit, this is referred to as the instrumental case (करण कारक karaṇ kārak).

When the postposition के लिये (ke liye) is used in the sense of 'for the purpose of', the postposition can be dropped and the oblique is retained: e.g., I am going to the park [to stroll]: मैं घूमने पार्क जा रही हूँ। (maiṃ ghūmne pārk jā rahī hūṃ.) When the postposition के लिये (ke liye) is used in another sense, it can never be dropped with the retention of oblique.

Examples:

He covered his face / with the bedsheet. (Bismillāh)
instrument

चादर से / उसने मुँह ढँक लिया। (cādar se usne muṃh ḍhaṃk liyā.)
Instr. (Obl. + से)

I had my greetings sent / through the servant. (Bismillāh)
instrument

मैंने / नौकर से / अपना सलाम भिजवाया। (maiṃne naukar se salām bhijvāyā.)
Instr. (Obl. + से)

"What is it?", Ṭinnū asked / very casually (*i.e., with great carelessness*). (Bismillāh)
circumstance

"क्या है?" टिन्नू ने / बड़ी बेपरवाही के साथ / पूछा। ("kyā hai?" ṭinnū baṛī beparvāhī ke sāth pūchā.)
circumstance (Obl. + के साथ)

"You too go / along with them." (Bismillāh)
circumstance

"तू भी / उनके साथ / चला जा। ("tū bhī unke sāth calā jā.)
circumstance (Obl. + के साथ)

I.2.3.3. OBLIQUE CASE USED AS A MARKER OF A POSSESSIVE RELATIONSHIP, IN COMBINATION WITH POSTPOSITION का (KĀ)

A word or word group followed by the postposition का (kā) 'of'/ 'belonging to' is used to indicate a relationship of possession between two nouns or between a noun and personal pronoun. This construction can occur in any constituent (subject, direct object, adjunct of place, etc.). The word group as a whole can thus be in the nominative or oblique case, as the postposition का (kā), contrary to any other postposition, is not necessarily the last word of the word group. In Sanskrit, the genitive case (संबंध कारक saṃbandh kārak) is used to express a possessive relationship.

The postposition का (kā) has two peculiar characteristics:

1. Syntactically, the word order is inverse to that in English when translating का (kā) as 'of' or 'belonging to', and instead uses the word order when apostrophe 's' ('s) would be used instead in English. E.g., my little brother's friends (Hindi word order) vs. 'the friends of my little brother'. As का (kā) is a postposition, and all the words that belong to the word group that precede a postposition always turn into oblique, words of the constituent that are placed before the का (kā) are put in the oblique case: 'my (obl.) little (obl.) brother (obl.)'s friends'.

2. का (kā) is a postposition in the sense that it turns the words that precede it into oblique; however, का (kā) behaves at the same time like an adjective, in the sense that it takes the gender and the number of the noun it qualifies. का (kā) can thus become का (kā), के (ke), or की (kī), regardless of whether it actually follows or precedes the noun it ties to the possessor. In the example of 'my father's book' (i.e., 'the book of my father'), the 'of' would be की (kī), i.e., feminine and singular, as 'book' is feminine and singular, and the gender of the possessor (father) is irrelevant for the gender of की (kī) 'of'.

Examples:

It / was / a village of farmers. (Premcand)

Pred. Nom का: m., because referring to 'village', being m. sg. (Predicate)

किसानों का गाँव / था। (kisānoṃ kā gāṃv thā)

Obl. + का in Nom. m. sg (Pred.)

I am the daughter of the *mulla* of the mosque. (Ugra)

Pred. Nom.

मैं / मस्जिद के मुल्ला की बेटी / हूँ। (maiṃ masjid ke *mullā* kī beṭī hūṃ.)

Nom f sg (Predicate): first के in obl. m. sg.: m. because referring to 'mullā', in obl. because followed by second की being f. sg. as it is referring to 'daughter'

That room / belonged to ('was') / 'of' Śhaśibālā. (Varmā)

Predicate

यह कमरा / शशिबाला का / था। (yah kamrā śaśibālā kā thā.)

Nom. (Obl. + का, m. because referring to 'room', being Nom. m. sg.) (Predicate)

He felt doubt / about the intention of Nathnī. (Gulzār)
Prepositional phrase

उसे / नथनी की नीयत पर / शक हुआ। (use nathnī kī nīyat par śak huā.)
Obl. + की because 'intention' is f. and obl., because followed by 'about' पर

The people saw that a very beautiful T.V.-set was placed / on the shoulder of that young man. (Bismillāh)
Prepositional phrase

लोगों ने देखा / उस नौजवान के कंधे पर / एक सुन्दर-सी टी.वी.सेट रखा था। (logoṃ ne dekhā us naujavān ke kandhe par ṭī.vī.seṭ rakhā thā.)
Place indication Obl. + के because 'shoulder' is m. sg. and obl., because followed by 'on' पर

I.2.3.4. OBLIQUE CASE USED AS A MARKER OF ORIGINATION OR DIRECTION, IN COMBINATION WITH POSTPOSITION को (KO) OR से (SE)

Word groups providing information about the person or object benefiting from the action described in the main verb but that are not the direct object of the sentence are followed by the postposition को (ko) 'to', 'at', or से (se). Sometimes, such a word (group) can be the indirect object. Many verbs of communication use the postposition को (ko) 'to', 'at', and/or 'from, with' से (se).

In Hindi, there are some verbs, named double causative verbs (see VI.7.) that can have two objects: they take both direct and indirect objects, as well as postpositional phrases to indicate origination or intermediary, and use the postposition को (ko) 'to', 'at', and/or 'from, with' से (se). In Sanskrit, two cases were used for such word groups: either the dative case (सम्प्रदान कारक sampradān kārak), or the ablative case (अपादान कारक apādān kārak). Another important function of the postposition से (se) in this respect is when it is used to make a comparison.

Examples:

In the crowd, people are asking / each other / questions. (Bismillāh)
Postpositional phrase in Hindi: "one from the other"

भीड़ में लोग / एक-दूसरे से / प्रश्न कर रहे हैं। (bhīṛ meṃ log ek-dūsre se praśn kar rahe haiṃ.)
Obl. + से. (lit.: 'one **from** the other')

For whom / do you have more love; / for me / or / for your friend? (Gulzār)
ind. obj. ind. obj. ind. obj.

तुम / किससे / ज़्यादा प्यार करते हो, / मुझसे / या / अपने दोस्त से? (tum kisse zyādā pyār
Obl. + से Obl. + से Obl. + से
karte ho, mujhse yā apne dost se?)

We both are giving you blessings / from the heart. (Premcand)
Abl. (origination)

हम दोनों / हृदय से / आशीर्वाद दे रहे हैं। (ham donoṃ hṛday se āśīrvād de rahe
Obl. + से
haiṃ.)

Saliva started to drip / from her mouth / just thinking this. (Gulzār)
Abl. (origination)

यह सोचके ही / उसके मुँह से / राल गिरने लगी। (yah socke hī uske muṃh se rāl girne
Obl. + से
lagī.)

Boys much smaller / than he / are bringing home VCRs. (Bismillāh)
Abl. (comparison)

उससे / छोटे-छोटे लड़के वी°सी°आर° उठाकर ला रहे हैं। (usse choṭe-choṭe laṛke vī.sī.ār.
Obl. + से
uṭhākar lā rahe haiṃ.)

The next night, I came / out of that house. (Ugra)
Abl. (origination)

अगली रात को मैं / उस घर से / बाहर निकल आई। (aglī rāt ko maiṃ us ghar se bāhar
Obl. + से
nikal āī.)

I.2.3.5. OBLIQUE CASE USED AS A MARKER OF LOCATIONS, IN COMBINATION WITH POSTPOSITION 'IN' में (MEṂ), 'ON' पर (PAR), 'UNTIL, UP TO' तक (TAK), ETC.

In this instance, the oblique is used to indicate a place. Often, Hindi uses postpositions like 'in' में (meṃ), 'on' पर (par), 'until, up to' तक (tak), etc. In Sanskrit, this function is fulfilled by the locative case (अधिकरण कारक adhikaraṇ kārak).

Examples:

There was exhilaration / in the atmosphere /, intoxication / in the air.
Loc. (place) Loc. (place)
(Premcand)

वहाँ के / वातावरण में / सरुर था / हवा में / नशा। (vahāṃ ke vātvaraṇ meṃ sarur thā,
Obl. + में Obl. + में
havā meṃ naśā.)

To wash their sin away, they bathe / in the Ganges. (Premcand)
Loc. (place)

अपने पाप को धोने के लिए / गंगा में / नहाते हैं। (apne pāp ko dhone ke lie gaṃgā
Obl. (place-name: no change) + में
meṃ nahāte haiṃ.)

You sit / on my back. (Gulzār)
Loc. (place)

तुम / मेरी पीठ पर / बैठ जाना। (tum merī pīṭh par baiṭh jānā.)
Obl. + पर

I.3. THE COMPOUND POSTPOSITIONS (परसर्ग PARSARG)

Hindi does not use prepositions, but postpositions. Many of these postpositions are compound. They consist of a noun or adverb, combined with the obl. of the genitive particle 'of': का (kā). I.e., when the noun is f., it will be 'की' (kī), and when the noun is m. sg. Obl. or m. pl., it will be 'के' (ke).

Note: Postpositions normally make the words that precede them and belong to the same word group oblique. However, when a compound postposition follows a personal pronoun, the pronoun combined with the obl. sg. m. के (ke) or obl. sg. f. की (kī) can fuse to a special form and become the possessive pronoun. E.g., I मैं (maiṃ) and the postposition 'near' के पास' (ke pās) does not become 'near I': 'मुझ (obl.) के पास' (mujh ke pās), but 'near me': मेरे पास (mere pās). (For more special forms, see IV.1.1.)

Some of the most frequently used postpositions are given on the next pages.

के अनुकूल (ke anukūl)	conformable to
के अनुसार (ke anusār)	according to
के अन्दर (ke andar)	in(side)
के अलावा (ke alāvā)	in addition, apart (from)
के आगे (ke āge)	in front of
के आस-पास (ke ās-pās)	near, around
के ऊपर (ke ūpar)	on top, above, over
के कारण (ke kāraṇ)	because of
(के) द्वारा (ke dvārā)	by means of
के निकट (ke nikaṭ)	near, close to
के नीचे (ke nīce)	under
के पश्चात (ke paścāt)	after(ward), behind
के पहले (ke pahle)	before (in time)
के पास (ke pās)	nearby, near
के पीछे (ke pīche)	behind
के पूर्व (ke pūrv)	before (in space)
के बदले (ke badle)	instead
के बाद (ke bād)	after
के बावजूद (ke bāvjūd)	notwithstanding
के बाहर (ke bāhar)	outside
(के) बिना (ke binā)	without
के बीच (ke bīc)	in between
के भीतर (ke bhītar)	within, inside
के मारे (ke māre)	because of
के लिए (ke lie)	for, on account of
(के) वास्ते (ke vāste)	because of
के विरुद्ध (ke viruddh)	against, hostile to
के समान (ke samān)	similar to, equal to
के समीप (ke samīp)	near, adjacent to
के सहारे (ke sahāre)	with the support of
के साथ(-साथ) (ke sāth-sāth)	together with

के सामने (ke sāmne)	in front of, before
के सिलसिले (ke silsile)	connected to
(के) सिवा (ke sivā)	apart from
की ओर (kī or)	in the direction of
की तरफ़ (kī taraf)	in the direction of
की तरह (kī tarah)	in the manner of

II. THE NOUN (संज्ञा SAṂGYĀ)

II.1. TABLE OF DECLENSION

Table 14. The noun: Table of declension

	MASCULINE		FEMININE	
	ENDING IN -Ā 'SON'	NOT ENDING IN -Ā 'OX'	ENDING IN -Ī 'DAUGHTER'	NOT ENDING IN -Ī 'SISTER'
Singular				
Nom.	बेटा (beṭā)	बैल (bail)	बेटी (beṭī)	बहन (bahan)
Obl.	बेटे (beṭe)	बैल (bail)	बेटी (beṭī)	बहन (bahan)
Voc.	बेटे (beṭe)	बैल (bail)	बेटी (beṭī)	बहन (bahan)
Plural				
Nom.	बेटे (beṭe)	बैल (bail)	बेटियाँ (betiyāṃ)	बहनें (bahaneṃ)
Obl.	बेटों (beṭoṃ)	बैलों (bailoṃ)	बेटियों (beṭiyoṃ)	बहनों (bahanoṃ)
Voc.	बेटो (beṭo)	बैलो (bailo)	बेटियो (beṭiyo)	बहनो (bahano)

To be able to decline a noun correctly, one needs to know the gender of the noun. Hindi has only two genders: masculine and feminine.

Masculine nouns are divided into two categories when it comes to their declension: they either end in -ā and follow the declension of बेटा (beṭā), or they do not end in -ā (this includes words ending in a consonant or any other vowel than -ā, including masculine nouns ending in -ī) and follow the declension of बैल (bail).

Feminine nouns are divided into two categories when it comes to their declension: they either end in -ī and follow the declension of बेटी (beṭī), or they do not end in -ī (this includes words ending in a consonant or any other vowel than -ī, including feminine nouns ending in -ā) and follow the declension of बहन (bahan).

Remarks:

1. Masculine tatsama[1] nouns that end in -ā follow the declension of बैल (bail) and not बेटा (beṭā). E.g., राजा (rājā) 'king', पिता (pitā) 'father'. The same is true for some tadbhava[2] nouns, especially kinship terms, e.g., चाचा (cācā) 'uncle'. Also, masculine nouns that were literally taken from Perso-Arabic and end in -ā will follow the declension of बैल (bail), e.g., दावा (dāvā) 'claim, lawsuit', सहरा (sahrā) 'desert'.

2. Masculine nouns ending in -i and -ī follow बैल (bail) but, in the obl. pl., the long -ī will become a short -i, followed by -y- (as is the case with feminine nouns on -ī). E.g., 'saint, ascetic': ऋषि (ṛṣi): Obl. pl. = ऋषियों (ṛṣiyoṃ); 'man': आदमी (ādmī): Obl. pl. = आदमियों (ādmiyoṃ).

For masculine nouns ending in -ū, the -ū will be shortened to u in the obl. pl., but no -y- is inserted. Sometimes, -v- is inserted. The -y- and -v- are semivowels that help to facilitate the pronunciation. The speaker will often insert them automatically. However, -v- is often not written. E.g., 'robber': डाकू (ḍākū): Obl. pl. = डाकुओं (ḍākuoṃ).

3. Feminine tatsama nouns ending in -ā follow the declension of the feminine nouns that do not end in -ī. Feminine tatsama nouns ending in -ī simply follow the declension of the feminine nouns that end in -ī. Words like माता (mātā) 'mother' and माला (mālā) 'garland' thus are declined like बहन (bahan) and become in Nom. pl. माताएँ (mātāeṃ), 'मालाएँ' (mālāeṃ). Words like देवी (devī) 'goddess' and नारी (nārī) 'woman' become in Nom. pl. देवियाँ (deviyāṃ), नारियाँ (nāriyāṃ).

4. Feminine nouns ending in short -i follow the declension of बेटी (beṭī). E.g., 'community, good birth': जाति (jāti): Nom. pl. = जातियाँ (jātiyāṃ), Obl. pl. = जातियों (jātiyoṃ).

5. Diminutives that end in -iyā are generally feminine. However, they do not follow the declension of the other feminine nouns that end in -ā, but follow their own pattern. E.g., 'little bird': Nom. sg. चिड़िया (ciṛiyā), Obl. sg. चिड़िया (ciṛiyā), Nom. pl. चिड़ियाँ (ciṛiyāṃ), Obl. pl. चिड़ियों (ciṛiyoṃ).

6. When an ending starting with a vowel is added to the noun, the

---

1. Cf. Part II: The Hindi Alphabet, note 6.
2. Cf. Part II: The Hindi Alphabet, note 6.

final long vowel will shorten. This is the case for all nouns (masculine and feminine) that end in a long vowel. A semivowel can be inserted between the two vowels, e.g., 'daughter- in-law': बहू (bahū), pl. बहुएँ (bahueṃ).

7. When a noun ends in a nasalized vowel and the ending that is added is also nasalized, the nasalization of the ending of the word in singular is dropped, e.g., 'flea': जूँ (jūṃ) becomes जुएँ (jueṃ). Masculine nouns ending in a nasalized -ā keep the nasalization in the Obl. sg. E.g., 'well': कुआँ (kuāṃ), Obl. sg = कुएँ (kueṃ); 'smoke': धुआँ (dhuāṃ), Obl. sg. = धुएँ (dhueṃ).

III. THE ADJECTIVE (विशेषण VIŚEṢAṆ)

III.1. TABLE OF DECLENSION

Table 15. The adjective: Table of declension

	ENDING IN -Ā: 'GOOD' अच्छा (ACCHĀ)		NOT ENDING IN -Ā: 'BEAUTIFUL' सुन्दर (SUNDAR)	
	MASCULINE	FEMININE	MASCULINE	FEMININE
Singular				
Nom.	अच्छा (acchā)	अच्छी (acchī)	सुन्दर (sundar)	सुन्दर (sundar)
Obl.	अच्छे (acche)	अच्छी (acchī)	सुन्दर (sundar)	सुन्दर (sundar)
Voc.	अच्छे (acche)	अच्छी (acchī)	सुन्दर (sundar)	सुन्दर (sundar)
Plural				
Nom.	अच्छे (acche)	अच्छी (acchī)	सुन्दर (sundar)	सुन्दर (sundar)
Obl.	अच्छे (acche)	अच्छी (acchī)	सुन्दर (sundar)	सुन्दर (sundar)
Voc.	अच्छे (acche)	अच्छी (acchī)	सुन्दर (sundar)	सुन्दर (sundar)

Examples:

अच्छा बेटा (acchā beṭā) 'a good son', अच्छी लड़की (acchī laṛkī) 'a good girl', सुन्दर बच्चा (sundar baccā) 'a beautiful child', काले कुत्ते (kāle kutte) 'black dogs', पीली क़लमें (pīlī qalameṃ) 'yellow pens', गुलाबी[1] कपड़े (gulābī kapṛe) 'pink clothes', अच्छे बेटों के लिए (acche beṭoṃ ke lie) 'for the good sons', अपने हाथों से (apne hāthoṃ se) 'with one's own hands', मीठी चाय में (mīṭhī cāy meṃ) 'in the sweet tea'.

Some of the adjectives are invariable, even if they end in -ā. When this is the case, it is indicated in the dictionary as '(inv.)'. The feminine forms of those adjectives thus also end in -ā, e.g., एक बंगला औरत (ek baṃglā aurat) 'a Bengālī woman', मेरी पसंदीदा फ़िल्म (merī pasandīdā film)

1. This is an invariable adjective on -ī and hence follows the declension of 'sundar'.

'my favorite movie'. So, they are the same in all forms ending in -ā, masculine or feminine, singular or plural. For example, दो बंगला आदमी (do baṃglā ādmī) 'two Bengālī men', मना फलों में (manā phaloṃ meṃ) 'in the forbidden fruits', वह पैदा हुई थी (vah paidā huī thī) 'she was born'.

As stated above, the genitive particle का (kā) behaves like an adjective. It agrees in gender and number with the noun. E.g., बेटे का घर (beṭe kā ghar) 'the house of the son', बेटे के घर में (beṭe ke ghar meṃ) 'in the house of the son', बेटों की माँ (beṭoṃ kī māṃ) 'the mother of the sons'.

IV. THE PRONOUNS (सर्वनाम SARVANĀM)

IV.1. TABLE OF DECLENSION

IV.1.1. PERSONAL (पुरुषवाचक सर्वनाम PURUĪVĀCAK SARVANĀM) AND POSSESSIVE PRONOUNS (स्वत्वबोधक सर्वनाम SVATVABODHAK SARVANĀM); अपना (APNĀ)

Table 16. Personal and possessive pronouns

	PERSONAL PRONOUNS			
	NOM./ने (NE)	OBL.	OBL. + को (KO) =	POSSESSIVE PRONOUNS
1 sg. I	मैं/मैं ने (maiṃ/maiṃ ne)	मुझ (mujh)	मुझे (mujhe)	मेरा (merā)
2 sg. you	तू/तू ने (tū/tū ne)	तुझ (tujh)	तुझे (tujhe)	तेरा (terā)
3 sg. he/she/ it/that/this	वह/उस ने (vah/us ne)	उस (us)	उसे (use)	उस का (us kā)
	यह/इस ने (yah/ is ne)	इस (is)	इसे (ise)	इस का (is kā)
1 pl. we	हम/हम ने (ham/ham ne)	हम (ham)	हमें (hameṃ)	हमारा (hamārā)
2 pl. you	तुम/तुम ने (tum/tum ne)	तुम (tum)	तुम्हें (tumheṃ)	तुम्हारा (tumhārā)
3 pl. they/ those/these	वे/उन्हों ने (ve/unhoṃ ne)	उन (un)	उन्हें (unheṃ)	उन का (un kā)
	ये/इन्हों ने (ye/inhoṃ ne)	इन (in)	इन्हें (inheṃ)	इन का (in kā)
you (hon.)	आप/आप ने (āp/āp ne)	आप (āp)	आप को (āp ko)	आप का (āp kā)

Oblique and possessive forms of personal pronouns are less confusing or unusual than generally first perceived by the English-speaking student. While many native speakers of English believe English does not have a case system left, it actually still displays case distinctions when it comes to personal pronouns. As is the case in Hindi, the personal pronouns in English, too, have special forms when preceded by a preposition, or by the possessive pronoun 'of': 'I' becomes 'from me', and 'of + I' becomes 'my'. Similarly, in Hindi, we find respectively मैं (maiṃ), मुझ से (mujh se), and मेरा (merā) (मैं + 'kā'), prepositions being postpositions in Hindi.

The reflexive pronoun अपना (apnā) 'one's own' can be used instead of the above possessive pronouns, when the subject of a sentence or a word group and the possessor are one and the same person. E.g., He is talking to his sister: वह अपनी बहन से बात कर रहा है। (vah apnī bahan se bāt kar rahā hai.). This stands in contrast to वह उसकी बहन से बात कर रहा है। (vah uskī bahan se bāt kar rahā hai.). In the first sentence, the word अपनी (apnī) indicates that the subject is talking to his own sister, where the word उसकी (uskī) in the second sentence indicates that the subject is talking to the sister of another person.

In case the main verb is an imperative, however, the word अपना (apnā) will refer to the person addressed and not the speaker, as the imperative does not have an explicit subject. E.g., Take your book!: अपनी किताब ले लो! (apnī kitāb le lo!). Here, अपनी (apnī) refers to the book of the person who is addressed.

When a word group is composite (i.e., 'my sister and I'), the possessive pronoun will never be replaced by अपना (apnā). E.g., उस ने मेरी बहन और मुझ को खाना दिया। (us ne merī bahan aur mujh ko khānā diyā) 'He gave food to my sister and me'; मेरी बहन और मैं घर गईं। (merī bahan aur maiṃ ghar gaīṃ) 'My sister and I went home'.

Remarks:

1. In the 1 and 2 sg. and pl., the personal pronoun is not put in the oblique case when followed by ने (ne). The personal pronouns of the 3 sg. and pl. do change into the oblique case: i.e., मैं ने (maiṃ ne), but उस ने (us ne), उन्हों ने (unhoṃ ne).

2. The forms in the column "Obl. + को" are words that are formed after fusion of the oblique form and the postposition को, hence the postposition को should not be added to these words. Apart from the fused forms मुझे (mujhe) and तुझे (tujhe), मुझ को (mujh ko) and तुझ को (tujh ko) are also used. उन को (un ko) and इन को (in ko) are used alongside the forms उन्हें (unheṃ) and इन्हें (inheṃ).

3. The 2 sg. तू (tū) is only used in very informal contexts, to address either a subordinate or a person with whom one has a very

close relationship (parents toward their children, lovers, or when praying or talking to God). When addressing someone with 'you', (i.e., someone of the same rank, age, and social background), one best uses the 2 pl. तुम (tum). The word तुम (tum) used for 'you' can refer to one individual or multiple people (interchangeable with तुम लोग (tum log) 'you people'), but is grammatically speaking always considered plural. One has to depend upon the context to be sure one or more persons are being addressed when तुम (tum) is used.

4. The forms in the column "Obl." are used whenever a postposition follows the pronoun. However, the postposition का (kā) is an exception to this rule, as the personal pronouns combined with the postposition का (kā) form the possessive pronouns as given in column 5. So: 'my' = 'of me' = I + का, in which case 'I' does not change into मुझ का (mujh kā), a form that does not exist, but becomes मेरा (merā).

5. Consequently, postpositions consisting of two words of which one is के (ke) or की (kī) will use the possessive pronoun: e.g., 'with me' becomes मेरे पास (mere pās) (= I + का in obl. because of the postposition पास). मुझ के पास (mujh ke pās) does not exist. In colloquial Hindi, one will often hear मेरे को (mere ko) instead of मुझे (mujhe). However, this is grammatically not correct in standard Hindi.

6. The postpositions का (kā), को (ko), and ने (ne) can be written attached to or separate from the personal pronoun, e.g., उन्होंने (unhoṃne) or उन्हों ने (unhoṃ ne), उसका (uskā) or उस का (us kā).

IV.1.2. DEMONSTRATIVE (संकेतवाचक SAṂKETVĀCAK), RELATIVE (संबंधवाचक SAMBANDHVĀCAK), INTERROGATIVE (प्रश्नवाचक PRAŚNVĀCAK), AND INDEFINITE (अनिश्चयवाचक ANIŚCAYVĀCAK) PRONOUNS (सर्वनाम SARVANĀM)

Table 17. Demonstrative, relative, interrogative, and indefinite pronouns

	SINGULAR			PLURAL		
	NOM.	OBL.	OBL. + को	NOM.	OBL./WITH ने	OBL. + को
this	यह (yah)	इस (is)	इसे (ise)	ये (ye)	इन/इन्हों (in(hoṃ))	इन्हें (inheṃ)
that	वह (vah)	उस (us)	उसे (use)	वे (ve)	उन/उन्हों (un(hoṃ))	उन्हें (unheṃ)
relative	जो (jo)	जिस (jis)	जिसे (jise)	जो (jo)	जिन/जिन्हों (jin(hoṃ))	जिन्हें (jinheṃ)
correl.	सो (so)	तिस (tis)	तिसे (tise)	सो (so)	तिन/तिन्हों (tin(hoṃ))	तिन्हें (tinheṃ)
who?	कौन (kaun)	किस (kis)	किसे (kise)	कौन (kaun)	किन/किन्हों (kin(hoṃ))	किन्हें (kinheṃ)
what?	क्या (kyā)	-	-	क्या (kyā)	-	-
some(one), any	कोई (koī)	किसी (kisī)	-	-	-	-
some, any (pl.)	-	-	-	कई (kaī)	कइयों (kaiyoṃ)	-
a little, some	कुछ (kuch)	कुछ (kuch)	-	कुछ (kuch)	कुछ (kuch)	-

Remarks: The enclitic particle ही (hī) is often used in combination with pronouns. Sometimes, these two words will fuse into a new word.

Examples:

वह + ही = वही (vah + hī= vahī) 'that specific one'

वहाँ + ही = वहीं (vahāṃ + hī= vahīṃ) 'right there'

उस + ही = उसी (से) (us + hī= usī) (se) 'because of him specifically'

उन्हों + ही = उन्हीं (से) (unhoṃ + hī= unhīṃ) (se) 'because of them specifically'

V. SYNTAX (वाक्यविन्यास VĀKYAVINYĀS)

Hindi is a subject-object-verb (SOV) language. As in most modern languages, the order of the syntax in Hindi is not fixed and there are many variants possible, especially in colloquial Hindi.

V.1. THE SYNTAX WITHIN ONE CONSTITUENT OF A SENTENCE

Generally speaking:

- The adjective is placed before the noun.
- The genitive construction (construction with the word का (kā)) has an inverse word order when compared to English. It actually follows the -'s construction (see I.2.3.3.).
- The postposition is always placed at the end of the word group.
- When a number is present in a word group that also includes a possessive pronoun and an adjective, the number generally follows the possessive pronoun.

Examples:

a bookshop = a shop of books
किताबों की दुकान (kitāboṃ kī dukān)

the brother of my friend = my friend's brother
मेरे दोस्त का भाई (mere dost kā bhāī)

in the direction of the fortress
क़िले की ओर / की तरफ़ (qile kī or / kī taraf)

my two good friends
मेरे दो अच्छे दोस्त (mere do acche dost)

V.2. THE SYNTAX WITHIN ONE SENTENCE

There are a few constituents that have a more or less fixed place in a sentence. Generally:

- The subject is placed at the beginning of the sentence (if the interrogative particle क्या (kyā) is not present).
- The verb is placed as the last word of the sentence (if the question tag न (na) 'isn't it' is not used).
- If used, the negative particle is placed right before the conjugated verb.[1]
- If an interrogative particle is used, it is placed right before the conjugated verb (and before the negative particle, if present) (see also V.3.).

In colloquial Hindi, the subject is often dropped when it only consists of a personal pronoun, or it is placed at the very end of the sentence, following the verb.

There are a few additional remarks about the adjunct of place and adjunct of time. Often, they are placed at the beginning of the sentence or following the subject. There is a subtle difference of emphasis between these two orders, as will become clear from the example below: भारत में शानदार इमारतें हैं। (bhārat meṃ śāndār imārateṃ haiṃ) vs. शानदार इमारतें भारत में हैं। (śāndār imārateṃ bhārat meṃ haiṃ). The first sentence, 'There are magnificent buildings in India', is a neutral, general statement about the architecture in India. The second sentence, 'The magnificent buildings are in India', is giving us more specific information regarding certain buildings, e.g., when looking at a picture.

---

1. Note that the notion of a conjugated verb can be interpreted in more than one way. In tenses where there are multiple compounds to the verbal tense, e.g., I am not eating, one could either say मैं खा नहीं रही हूँ। (maiṃ khā nahīṃ rahī hūṃ) or मैं नहीं खा रही हूँ। (maiṃ nahīṃ khā rahī hūṃ), depending upon whether or not one regards the stem खा (khā), which never changes, as part of the conjugated verb or not. The same flexibility in syntax can be applied to the interrogative particles. In my book *Tracing the Boundaries*, my research indicated that it is more common in Hindi to consider all constituents of the verbal tense as conjugated verb and place the negation/interrogative participle before the entire compound, whereas in Urdu, it is more likely to find them after the unconjugated stem or infinitive.

In the sentence डब्बे में सेब हैं। (ḍabbe meṃ seb haiṃ) vs. सेब डब्बे में हैं। (seb ḍabbe meṃ haiṃ), the same is true. The first sentence, 'There are apples in the box', is a neutral statement about the box. The second sentence, 'The apples are in the box', is more likely an answer to the question "Where are the apples?" Both sentences are grammatically correct, but the indication of place does not receive the same emphasis when moved.

Also note that when there are multiple place or time indications in one sentence, the broader indication comes first, followed by the more specific one(s), e.g., अगले साल जुलाई में मैं भारत जाऊँगी। (agle sāl julāī meṃ maiṃ bhārat jāūṃgī.) 'Next year, in July, I will go to India'.

Examples:

That same day I collected all my jewelry, and the next night, I left that house.

उसी दिन मैंने अपने सब गहने एकत्र कर लिए और अगली रात को मैं उस घर से बाहर निकल आई। (Ugra)

(usī din maiṃne apne sab gahne ekatra kar lie aur aglī rāt ko maiṃ us ghar se bāhar nikal āī.)

At that moment, wrinkles will appear on your face. (Varmā)[2]

उस समय तुम्हारे मुख पर झुर्रियाँ पड़ जाएँगी। (us samay tumhāre mukh par jhurriyāṃ paṛ jāeṃgī.)

In a valley in Kashmir, on the bank of the river Jhelum, there is a lush, green jungle. (Gulzār) (Note: multiple place indications, going from broader to more specific.)

कश्मीर की एक वादी में दरियाये झेलम के किनारे एक हरा भरा जंगल है। (kaśmīr kī ek vādī meṃ dariyāye jhelam ke kināre ek harā bharā jaṃgal hai.)

Come right under this very tree every day at noon. (Gulzār)

रोज़ दोपहर को इसी पेड़ के नीचे आ जाया कर। (roz dopahar ko isī peṛ ke nīce ā jāyā kar.)

2. The context is that a man is talking to a single woman, predicting her life in old age, using the plural to show respect.

There was no shortage of work in the village. (Premcand)
गाँव में काम की कमी नहीं थी। (gāṃv meṃ kām kī kamī nahīṃ thī.)

So then you will come to my house this evening to eat, won't you? (Gulzār)
तो फिर आज शाम को मेरे घर पर खाने को आओगे न? (to phir āj śām ko mere ghar par khāne ko āoge, na?)

What do we call that? (Yaśpāl)
क्या कहते हैं उसे? (kyā kahte haiṃ use?)

V.3. INTERROGATIVE PARTICLES

Interrogative adjectives

कितना? (kitnā)	how many?
कैसा? (kaisā)	how? what kind of?
कौन-सा? (kaun-sā)	what? which?

Interrogative pronouns

कब? (kab)	when?
कहाँ? (kahāṃ)	where?
किधर? (kidhar)	whither/in which direction?
कौन? (kaun)	who?
क्या? (kyā)	what (kind of)?
क्यों? (kyoṃ)	why?

Generally, interrogative particles are placed right before the conjugated verb.

Examples:

Where are you coming from? (Ugra)
तू कहाँ से आ रही है? (tū kahāṃ se ā rahī hai?)

Mister Crocodile, why are you crying? (Gulzār)
मियाँ मगरमछ रो क्यों रहे हो? (miyāṃ magarmach ro kyoṃ rahe ho?)

[If] you don't take revenge for him, who will? (Ugra)
उसका बदला तू न लेगा तो कौन लेगा? (uskā badlā tū na legā to kaun legā?)

When will [we] get a better opportunity than this one? (Ugra)
इससे अच्छा अवसर कब मिलेगा? (isse acchā avsar kab milegā?)

But which answer will you give to the people?[3] (Premcand)
लेकिन लोगों को जवाब क्या दोगे? (lekin logoṃ ko javāb kyā doge?)

Why did you not give me *(pl. used for respect)* a shroud? (Premcand)
तुमने हमें क़फ़न क्यों नहीं दिया? (tumne hameṃ kafan kyoṃ nahīṃ diyā?)

There are three possible exceptions to this rule. The interrogative particle क्या (kyā) has two different functions. When क्या (kyā) is placed before the verb, it is translated as the interrogative 'what?'. However, when a yes-no question is asked, क्या (kyā) is placed at the beginning of the sentence. When a sentence starts with क्या (kyā), the particle stays untranslated and represents the inversion (putting the verb before the subject) one finds in English.

Examples:

Was it me who had murdered my husband? (Ugra)
क्या मैंने ही अपने पति की हत्या की थी? (kyā maiṃne hī apne pati kī hatyā kī thī?)

Do you live here somewhere? (Varmā)
क्या आप यहीं कहीं रहते हैं? (kyā āp yahīṃ kahīṃ rahte haiṃ?)

The other two possible exceptions are the interrogative particles कितना (kitnā) 'how many' and कैसा (kaisā)/कौन-सा (kaun-sā) 'how/what kind of'.[4] While all the other interrogative participles are invariable, these two are adjectives. They will take the gender and the number of the noun or personal pronoun they refer to.

3. क्या (kyā) means 'what', hence the more literal translation would be "What will you answer the people?"
4. Sometimes one can come across क्या (kyā) used in the same sense, e.g., प्यारी देखो मैं तुम्हारे लिए क्या तोहफ़ा लाया हूँ। (pyārī, dekho maiṃ tumhāre lie kyā tohfā lāyā hūṃ) (Gulzār): Darling, look what treat I have brought for you.

Examples:

How are you? (when addressing a man)
आप कैसे हैं? (āp kaise haiṃ?)

How are you? (when addressing a woman)[5]
आप कैसी हैं? (āp kaisī haiṃ?)

[I] don't know what kind of charm of her Naththu liked. (Meaning: "I don't know what in her attracted him") (Gulzār)
पता नहीं नथ्थु को उसकी कौनसी अदा भा गई। (patā nahīṃ naththu ko uskī kaunsī adā bhā gaī.)

कैसा (kaisā)/कौन-सा (kaun-sā) (how? what kind of?) and कितना (kitnā) (how many?) can be used as adjectives, combined with a noun.

Examples:

What kind of fruit is this?
यह कैसा फल है? (yah kaisā phal hai?)

How many books are there in this box?
इस डब्बे में कितनी किताबें हैं? (is ḍabbe meṃ kitnī kitābeṃ haiṃ?)

Sometimes, interrogative particles are put at the beginning of a sentence when they are used in an affirmative sense.

Example:

Natthu narrated the entire history. Why and how the friendship with Lālū had arisen. (Gulzār)
नथ्थु ने सारी राम कहानी[6] कह दी। क्यों और कैसे लालू से यारी हुई। (naththu ne sārī rām kahānī kah dī. kyoṃ aur kaise lālū se yārī huī.)

---

5. In some regions, Hindi speakers feel that using the feminine adjective or verbal forms for women of high status is disrespectful. They will use the masculine form to show respect toward women they consider to be their superior.
6. Literally, 'the entire Rām story'. This is a reference to the *Rāmāyana*, implying that it is a long and complicated story.

V.4. RELATIVE (संबंधवाचक शब्द SAMBANDHVĀCAK ŚABD) CORRELATIVE CONJUNCTIONS (सह-संबंधित शब्द SAH-SAMBANDHIT ŚABD)

Table 18. Relative-correlative conjunctions

RELATIVE	(POSSIBLE) CORRELATIVES
जो (jo) the one who, which	वह/वे (vah/ve) that, he, she, it, they
	यह/ये (yah, ye) this, he, she, it, they
	सो (so)[1] = वह (vah)
जैसा (jaisā; adj.) like, of such a sort as	ऐसा (aisā; adj.) of this sort
	वैसा (vaisā; adj.) of that sort
	तैसा (taisā; adj.) of that sort
जितना (jitnā; adj.) as many/much as	इतना (itnā; adj.) as much/many
	उतना (utnā; adj.) as much/many
जब (jab) when	तब (tab) then
	तो (to) then
अगर (agar) if	तब (tab) then
	तो (to) then
जब भी (jab bhī)/जभी (jabhī) whenever	तब भी (tab bhī)/तभी (tabhī) then
जहाँ (jahāṃ) where	यहाँ (yahāṃ) there
	वहाँ (vahāṃ) there
	तहाँ (tahāṃ) there
जिधर (jidhar) in whichever direction	इधर (idhar) over here
	उधर (udhar) over there
ज्यों (jyoṃ) just as, in the way in which	यों (yoṃ) in the same way
	त्यों (tyoṃ) in the same way
क्योंकि (kyoṃki) because	इस लिए (is lie) therefore

[1] सो is used less frequently. Cf. the proverb जो होगा सो होगा (jo hogā so hogā): "*que sera, sera*."

In English, the use of subordinate and correlative conjunctions is more limited than in Hindi. Subordinating conjunctions include 'the one who', 'the thing that', 'if', 'because', 'provided', etc. Whenever such conjunctions are used, two clauses or phrases will be connected. Correlative and subordinate conjunctions connect, grammatically speaking, two independent sentences. Contrary to English, in Hindi the correlative conjunction is mostly expressed. If one conjunction remains implicit, it will be the relative conjunction. This is initially somewhat puzzling for English-speakers. For example, the English sentence "The book you see over there is my brother's" will change in Hindi to "Which book you see over there, that is my brother's": जो किताब तुम वहाँ देखते हो वह मेरे भाई की है। (jo kitāb tum vahāṃ dekhte ho, vah mere bhāī kī hai.).

Examples:

In the late afternoon, when I usually went for a walk, then Ms. Shaśibālādevī could also be seen walking. (Varmā)

सन्ध्या के समय जब मैं टहलने के लिए जाया करता था तो श्रीमती शशिबालादेवी प्रायः टहलती हुई दिखाई देती थीं[7]। (sandhyā ke samay jab maiṃ ṭahalne ke lie jāyā kartā thā to śrīmatī śaśibālādevī prāyaḥ ṭahaltī huī dikhāī detī thīṃ.)

Let the mystery remain the way it is. (Lit.: 'That mystery the way in which it is, thus let it remain.') (Varmā)

यह रहस्य जैसा है वैसा ही रहने दो। (yah rahasya jaisā hai vaisā hī rahne do.)

Therefore, I will give you something that would support you in those days. (Lit.: 'Therefore I will gift you that thing which would do your job in those days.')[8] (Varmā)

इसलिए मैं तुम्हें वह चीज़ प्रेज़ेण्ट करूँगा जो उन दिनों तुम्हारे काम आवे। (islie maiṃ tumheṃ vah cīz prezeṇṭ karūṃgā jo un dinoṃ tumhāre kām āve.)

Whose face I've never seen, today I would see her uncovered body? (Lit.: Whose face I've never seen, today her uncovered body I would see?) (Premcand)

---

7. Note that the verb appears in feminine plural to show respect.
8. The context is that a man is talking to a single woman, predicting her life in old age, using the plural to show respect.

जिसका कभी मुँह नहीं देखा आज उसका उघड़ा हुआ बदन देखूँ। (jiskā kabhī muṃh nahīṃ dekhā āj uskā ughṛā huā badan dekhūṃ?)

He was such a man who sometimes spoke a couple of nice words to me. (Ugra)

वही ऐसा आदमी था जो कभी मुझसे दो-चार मीठी बातें करता। (vahī aisā ādmī thā jo kabhī mujhse do-cār mīṭhī bāteṃ kartā.)

Opposite the alley where there used to be a very high beam, there was now a three-story-high building. (Rākeś)

गली के सामने जहाँ पहले ऊंचे-ऊंचे शहतीर रखे रहते थे वहाँ अब एक तिमंजिला मकान खड़ा था। (galī ke sāmne jahāṃ pahle ūṃce-ūṃce śahtīr rakhe rahte the vahāṃ ab ek timanzilā makān khaṛā thā.)

V.5. THE DEGREES OF COMPARISON

The comparative degree (उत्तरावस्था uttarāvasthā): In most cases, instead of a comparative adjective ('taller', 'smaller') or adverb, the positive or base form is used ('tall', 'small'). When comparing two objects/persons, the referent (the one to which the other is compared) is followed by the postposition से (se). Generally, but not always, the object/person one is comparing is placed first, followed by the referent joined by the postposition से (se). Next, the quality or characteristic that is being compared is expressed with the positive adjective or adverb. Of course, the adjective agrees in number and gender with the grammatical subject, the person/object that is compared, not the referent.

Example:

A temple (the object one is comparing: X) is bigger (the quality or characteristic) than a house (the referent: Y).

मन्दिर (X) घर (Y) से बड़ा है। (mandir ghar se baṛā hai.)

One could translate 'a temple (मन्दिर mandir) is (है hai) big (बड़ा baṛā, agreeing with 'temple') compared to (से se) a house (घर ghar)'. The adverb 'more' अधिक (adhik) or ज़्यादा (zyādā) can be added before the adjective.

Examples:

I consider the words of my mother more holy than the verses of the Qur'ān. (Ugra)

मैं अपनी माँ की बातों को क़ुरान शरीफ़ की आयतों से अधिक पवित्र मानता हूँ। (maiṃ apnī māṃ kī bātoṃ ko qurān śarīf kī āyatoṃ se adhik pavitr māntā hūṃ.)

To tell the truth, I never in my life saw a more low and selfish crocodile than Nathnī. (Gulzār)

सच कहूँ तो मैंने अपनी ज़िन्दगी में नथनी से ज़्यादा कमीनी और ख़ुदग़र्ज़ मगरमछ नहीं देखी। (sac kahūṃ to maiṃne apnī zindagī meṃ nathnī se zyādā kamīnī aur khudgarz magarmach nahīṃ dekhī.)

I have eaten more than twenty [*pūrīs*]. (Premcand)

बीस [पूरियों] से ज़्यादा खाई थीं। (bīs [pūriyoṃ] se zyādā khāī thīṃ.)

The superlative degree (उत्तमावस्था uttamāvasthā): The base form is used, rather than a superlative adjective ('tallest', 'smallest') or adverb in this construction as well. The referent + से (se) from the comparative construction is replaced by the words सब से (sab se) 'of all', which is followed by the positive adjective or adverb, and the verb. The adjective agrees in number and gender with the grammatical subject, the person/object that is compared, not the referent.

Examples:

This building (the object: X) is the highest (quality) of all (the referent: सब से).

यह इमारत (X) सब से ऊंची है। (yah imārat sab se ūṃcī hai.)

Even in death, she fulfilled our biggest desire in life. (Premcand)

मरते-मरते हमारी ज़िन्दगी की सबसे बड़ी लालसा पूरी कर गई। (marte-marte hamārī zindagī kī sabse baṛī lālsā pūrī kar gaī.)

V.6. THE VERB 'TO HAVE'

The verb 'to have' cannot simply be translated with a verb in Hindi. To indicate that someone possesses something, three different categories of possessions are distinguished, which each call for a specific postposition following the possessor. The verb used is always 'to be'.[9]

1. Inalienable possessions: This category comprises family members, body parts, and real estate (houses, shops, villages). To translate the verb 'to have' in connection with any of such possessions, one should use the postposition का (kā) following the possessor.

Examples:

The girl has only one hand.
लड़की का सिर्फ़ एक ही हाथ है। (laṛkī kā sirf ek hī hāth hai.)

The landowner has (owns) two villages.
जमीनदार के दो गाँव हैं। (zamīndār ke do gāṃv haiṃ.)

I have had nine sons. (Premcand)
मेरे नौ लड़के हुए। (mere nau laṛke hue.)

2. Material possessions: To express the verb 'to have' when it comes to material possessions, the postposition के पास (ke pās) follows the possessor. Note that time also falls into this category; after all, time is money.

Examples:

I don't have money.
मेरे पास पैसे नहीं हैं। (mere pās paise nahīṃ haiṃ.)

The old woman has a lot of books.
बूढ़ी औरत के पास बहुत-सी किताबें हैं। (būṛhī aurat ke pās bahut-sī kitābeṃ haiṃ.)

The doctor does not have time.
डाक्टर के पास समय नहीं है। (dākṭar ke pās samay nahīṃ hai.)

---

9. Note that we are talking about the verb 'to have'; if one wants to say "these books are his," there is no need to use any of the following constructions.

3. Abstract possessions: Feelings, pain, happiness, etc., are considered abstract possessions. To translate the verb 'to have', the postposition को (ko) is used, following the possessor. (See also V.7.1.)

Examples:

He knows (lit.: '[it] is known to him').
उसको मालूम है। (usko mālūm hai.)

I have a headache.
मुझे सिरदर्द है। (mujhe sirdard hai.)

V.7. FEELINGS AND SOME SPECIAL VERBS

V.7.1. FEELINGS AND EMOTIONS: लगना (LAGNĀ), आना (ĀNĀ), AND होना (HONĀ)

In Hindi, one can find constructions parallel to English in which the emotion or sensation is expressed by an adjective used predicatively ("the child is hungry"). Often such feelings are expressed in an indirect way, using a noun to describe the emotion or physical sensation. Many feelings and emotions are constructed as an abstract possession (see V.6.3).

Apart from the verb होना (honā) 'to be', the verbs लगना (lagnā) 'to be attached to, to become fixed on, to be felt by' and आना (ānā) 'to come' are often used. These verbs combined with the postposition को (ko) following the experiencer can be used to express a feeling, emotion, or state of mind. A few such verbs are चिन्ता होना (cintā honā) 'to worry', डर लगना (ḍar lagnā) 'to be afraid', भूख लगना (bhūkh lagnā) 'to feel hungry', खुशी होना (khuśī honā) 'to feel happy'. The verbs लगना (lagnā) and होना (honā) can be put in different tenses, e.g., the continuous tense to emphasize that a feeling or sensation is being experienced at that moment, the perfective tense to express that an emotion or sensation has attached itself to somebody and hence is being experienced now, the imperfective tense to describe a more constant condition or emotion.

Examples:

I am hungry. (Lit.: 'hunger is attached to me')
मुझे भूख लगी है। (mujhe bhūkh lagī hai.)

He used to enjoy doing this a lot. (Gulzār)
उसे ऐसा करने में बहुत मज़ा आता था। (use aisā karne meṃ bahut mazā ātā thā.)

Will he like such things?
क्या उसको ऐसी चीज़ें पसन्द आएँगी? (kyā usko aisī cīzeṃ pasand āeṃgī?)

Meeting each other and talking, the people were feeling very happy. (Rākeś)
मिलकर और बातें करके लोगों को बहुत खुशी हो रही थी। (milkar aur bāteṃ karke logoṃ ko bahut khuśī ho rahī thī.)

I (f.) will be so satisfied! (Ugra)
मुझे उतना ही संतोष होगा। (mujhe utnā hī santoṣ hogā.)

While the combination with होना (honā) or आना (ānā) is intransitive, indirect, and describes a state, e.g., विश्वास होना (viśvās honā) 'to be sure, have faith', some of those verbs can also be combined with the verb करना (karnā), to render them transitive, more active, or direct, e.g., विश्वास करना (viśvās karnā) 'to have confidence, to believe in'. When करना (karnā) is the main verb, the subject in English and Hindi will be the same.

Examples:

The people will not believe [us]. (Premcand)
लोगों को विश्वास न आयेगा। (logoṃ ko viśvās na āyegā.) ('belief will not come to the people') could be changed to: लोग हम पर विश्वास नहीं करेंगे। (log ham par viśvās nahīṃ kareṃge.)

My wife only liked cows' milk, not buffalos'. (Bismillāh)
मेरी बीवी गाय का ही दूध पसन्द करती थी भैंस का नहीं। (merī bīvī gāy kā hī dūdh pasand kartī thī, bhaiṃs kā nahīṃ.)

V.7.1.1. लगना (LAGNĀ) 'TO SEEM'

The verb लगना (lagnā) is used in the sense of 'to seem'. In this case, the emotion will generally be expressed with an adjective instead of a noun. If को (ko) is used, it follows the observer, not the person experiencing the sensation.

Examples:

The women seem distressed.
औरतें परेशान लगती हैं। (auratem̩ pareśān lagtī haim̩.)

It seems to me that the women are distressed.
मुझे लगता है कि औरतें परेशान हैं। (mujhe lagtā hai ki auratem̩ pareśān haim̩.)

V.7.1.2. लगना (LAGNĀ) 'TO LIKE' AND 'TO DISLIKE'

लगना (lagnā) can be used to express 'to like' अच्छा लगना (acchā lagnā) and 'to dislike' बुरा लगना (burā lagnā). Note that the adjective and infinitive will take the gender and number of the object that is liked or disliked, while the experiencer is followed by को (ko).

Example:

The boy likes to study Hindi.
लड़के को हिन्दी पढ़नी अच्छी लगती है। (lar̩ke ko hindī par̩hnī acchī lagtī hai.)

The verbs दिल लगना (dil lagnā) and मन लगना (man lagnā) can also be used to express 'to like'. However, they are often not interchangeable with अच्छा लगना (acchā lagnā). Looking at the literal translation of दिल / मन लगना (dil/man lagnā), it becomes evident that the verbs are used to express that 'one's heart is (not) in it', or 'one does (not) feel like' something. The verbs दिल and मन लगाना (dil/man lagānā) is used to express 'to put one's heart/soul into something', 'to do something with motivation'.

Examples:

I am tired. I do not feel like watching a movie.

मैं थक गई हूँ। फ़िल्म देखने में मन नहीं लगता है। (maiṃ thak gaī hūṃ. film dekhne meṃ man nahīṃ lagtā hai.)

Daughter, study with motivation. (Lit.: Study, putting your heart into it.)

बेटी, मन लगाकर पढ़ो। (beṭī, man lagākar paṛho.)

V.7.1.3. लगना (LAGNĀ) 'TO BE EXPENDED'; 'TO TAKE (TIME, ENERGY, COST)'

Another notable use of the verb लगना (lagnā) is to express how much time or money something will take. The action described is followed by the postposition में (meṃ).

Examples:

It takes two hours to get to Delhi.

दिल्ली जाने में दो घण्टे लगते हैं। (dillī jāne meṃ do ghaṇṭe lagte haiṃ.)

It will cost a lot of money to go to India.

हिन्दुसतान जाने में बहुत पैसे लगेंगे। (hindustān jāne meṃ bahut paise lageṃge.)

V.7.2. THE VERB मिलना (MILNĀ)

मिलना (milnā) can be found in combination with two different postpositions, which determine its meaning. When combined with the postposition को (ko), मिलना (milnā) is translated as 'to obtain, to get, to be received'. In that case, the English subject will be followed by the postposition को (ko), and the direct object of the English sentence will become the subject of the Hindi sentence.

Examples:

The man receives a lot of gifts.

आदमी को बहुत भेंटें मिलती हैं। (ādmī ko bahut bheṃṭeṃ miltī haiṃ.)

She will receive your letter.

उसको तुम्हारा पत्र मिलेगा। (usko tumhārā patr milegā.)

However, when the verb मिलना is combined with से, it means 'to meet with', and the English subject and Hindi subject will be the same.

Example:

The man will meet (with) the woman.

आदमी औरत से मिलेगा। (ādmī aurat se milegā.)

V.8. OBLIGATIONS: 'HAVE TO', 'SHOULD', 'NEED'

V.8.1. चाहिए (CĀHIE) 'IT IS DESIRABLE, WANTED, NEEDED'

Infinitive	+	चाहिए (cāhie)	=	'ought to', 'should', 'need to'

Infinitive + चाहिए (cāhie): this combination expresses an obligation or need.[10] Often, the obligation is a moral one. The constituent of the sentence that would be the subject in English is followed by को (ko) in Hindi, and hence it cannot be the grammatical subject. As a result, when there is an object to the main verb (i.e., the main verb is a transitive infinitive), this object will become the grammatical subject, and the main verb (i.e., the infinitive) will agree in number and gender with this object when the object is not followed by को (ko).

To express an obligation in the past, the past tense of होना (honā) can be added. If the infinitive agrees, the past form of होना (honā) will also agree. When the infinitive does not agree, it will appear in the 3 m. sg.

If the main clause contains चाहिए (cāhie), it is followed by कि (ki); the subordinate clause following the कि (ki) will often be put in the subjunctive.

Examples:

Upon dying, she ought to have a new shroud. (Premcand)

उसे मरने पर नया कफ़न चाहिए। (use marne par nayā kafan cāhie.)

I (m./f.) should read that book.

मुझे उस किताब को पढ़ना चाहिए। (mujhe us kitāb ko paṛhnā cāhie.)

---

10. This is a historic passive form of the verb चाहना (cāhnā) and never changes when used in this sense.

The feeling arose to him that he should not say this thing. (Rākeś)

उसे एहसास हो आया कि यह बात उसे नहीं कहनी चाहिए। (use ehsās ho āyā ki yah bāt use nahīṃ kahnī cāhie.)

It is necessary for him/her to do this.

उसको चाहिए कि ऐसा करे। (usko cāhie ki vah aisā kare.)

The girl ought to be married off right now. (Bismillāh)

लड़की की शादी अब कर ही देनी चाहिए। (laṛkī kī śādī ab kar hī denī cāhie.)

V.8.2. पड़ना (PAṚNĀ) 'TO HAVE TO'

Infinitive	+	पड़ना (paṛnā)	=	'to have to', 'must'

Infinitive + पड़ना (paṛnā): This construction is used to express an obligation or compulsion, often coming from an external source. Here too, the constituent of the sentence that would be the subject in English, is followed by को (ko) and hence cannot be the grammatical subject in Hindi. As a result, when there is an object to the main verb (i.e., the main verb is a transitive infinitive),[11] this object will become the grammatical subject and the main verb (i.e., the infinitive) will agree in number and gender with this object when the object is not followed by को (ko). The verb पड़ना (paṛnā) can be put in the imperfective, future, subjunctive, or perfective tense.

Examples:

Children have to go to the dentist once a year.

बच्चों को साल में एक बार दन्तचिकित्सक के पास जाना पड़ता है। (baccoṃ ko sāl meṃ ek bār dantcikitsak ke pās jānā paṛtā hai.)

I will be compelled to take legal action. (Bismillāh)[12]

मुझे कानूनी कार्रवाई करने के लिए बाध्य होना पड़ेगा। (mujhe kānūnī kārravāī karne ke lie bādhy honā paṛegā.)

---

11. From a grammatical point of view, there are two kind of verbs: transitive and intransitive. See VI.3.2. for an explanation of transitivity and intransivity.
12. This example is taken from the short story आधा फूल आधा शव (ādhā phūl ādhā śav) from the collection Bismillāh, *Athiti devo bhav*.

Will the university have to change their syllabi too? (Bismillāh)[13]

क्या विश्वविद्यालय को उनके पाठक्रम भी अलग-अलग बनाने पड़ेंगे। (kyā viśvavidyālay ko unke pāṭhkram bhī alag-alag banāne paṛeṃge?)

You had to read those books.

तुम्हें वे किताबें पढ़नी पड़ती थीं। (tumheṃ ve kitābeṃ paṛhnī paṛtī thīṃ.)

V.8.3. होना (HONĀ) 'TO HAVE TO'

Infinitive	+	होना (honā)	=	'to have to', 'must'

Infinitive + होना (honā): This construction is similar to the obligation expressed by the infinitive combined with पड़ना (paṛnā) or चाहिए (cāhie). Often, the construction with पड़ना (paṛnā) is considered to be slightly stronger than the one expressed with होना (honā). The construction is identical to that of the other obligations, in that the subject in English is followed by को (ko). The infinitive is followed by a conjugated form of होना (honā).

Examples:

I have to help my sister.

मुझे मेरी बहन की मदद करनी है। (mujhe merī bahan kī madad karnī hai.)

Now [I] will have to stay in the house for a few more days. (Varmā)

अभी कुछ दिन घर में और ठहरना होगा। (abhī kuch din ghar meṃ aur ṭhaharnā hogā.)

I had to work till midnight.

मुझे रात को बारह बजे तक काम करना था। (mujhe rāt ko bārah baje tak kām karnā thā.)

13. This example is taken from the short story आधा फूल आधा शव (ādhā phūl ādhā śav) from the collection Bismillāh, *Athiti devo bhav*.

VI. THE VERB (क्रिया KRIYĀ)

VI.1. TENSES AND ASPECTS

There are three verbal tenses in Hindi: present, past, and future. Apart from these tenses, there is a grammatical distinction between the different aspects of the verb; there are actions that are complete (perfective), incomplete or expressing a habit (imperfective), and ongoing (continuous). Aspect and tense are combined, e.g., incomplete actions can take place in the present or past; past tenses can be combined with different aspects (perfective, imperfective, continuous), each with their specific usage.

VI.2. FORMATION

Table 19. The verb: Formation

	STEM +	EXAMPLE: बोल- (BOL-) 'TO SPEAK'	
Infinitive[1]	- ना (nā)	बोलना (bolnā) 'to speak'	
Imperative	- इए (ie)/इये (iye) (polite imperative)	बोलिए/बोलिये (bolie/boliye) 'speak please'	
	- ओ (o) (informal imperative)	बोलो (bolo) 'speak'	
	- ∅ (familiar; restrictions apply!)[2]	बोल (bol) 'speak'	
	- ना (nā) (general imp.)	बोलना (bolnā) 'speak' (to a group)	
	- इएगा (iegā) (inv.) (very polite; *idem.* usage of Subjunctive)	बोलिएगा (boliegā) 'speak please'	
Absolutive	- ∅	बोल (bol)	'speaking or having spoken'
	- कर (kar)	बोलकर (bolkar)	
	- के (ke)	बोलके (bolke)	
Verbal noun	-नेवाला (-nevālā)	बोलनेवाला (bolnevālā) 'he who speaks'	
Subjunctive	-ऊँ (ūṃ) (1 m./f. sg.)	बोलूँ (bolūṃ) 'I would speak'	
	-ए (e) (2 & 3 m./f. sg.)	बोले (bole) 'you/he/she would speak'	
	-एँ (eṃ) (1 & 3 m./f. pl.)	बोलें (boleṃ) 'we/they/you (formal) would speak'	
	-ओ (o) (2 m./f. pl.)	बोलो (bolo) 'you would speak'	

Table 19. The verb: Formation *(continued)*

	STEM +	EXAMPLE: बोल- (BOL-) 'TO SPEAK'
Future	- 1, 2, 3 sg. Subj. + -गा (gā) (= 1, 2, 3 m. sg.)	बोलूँगा (bolūṃgā) 'I will speak', बोलेगा (bolegā) 'you will speak', बोलेगा, (bolegā) 'he will speak'
	- 1, 2, 3 pl. Subj. + -गे (ge) (=1, 2, 3 m. pl.)	बोलेंगे (boleṃge) 'we will speak', बोलोगे (bologe) 'you will speak', बोलेंगे (boleṃge) 'they will speak'
	- 1, 2, 3 sg. Subj. + -गी (gī) (= 1, 2, 3 f. sg.)	बोलूँगी (bolūṃgī) 'I will speak', बोलेगी (bolegī) 'you will speak', बोलेगी (bolegī) 'she will speak'
	- 1, 2, 3 pl. Subj. + -गी (gī) (= 1, 2, 3 f. pl.)	बोलेंगी (boleṃgī) 'we will speak', बोलोगी (bologī) 'you will speak', बोलेंगी (boleṃgī) 'they will speak'
Present participle	- ता (tā) (m. sg)	बोलता (boltā) 'speaking'
	- ती (tī) (f. sg./pl.)	बोलती (boltī)
	- ते (te) (m. pl.)	बोलते (bolte)
	- तीं (tīṃ) (f. pl.: **only used when the Prs. part. is used without a form of 'to be' present**)	बोलतीं (boltīṃ)
Past participle	- आ (ā) (m. sg.)	बोला (bolā) 'spoken'
	- ए (e) (m. pl.)	बोले (bole)
	- ई (ī) (f. sg./pl.)	बोली (bolī)
	- ईं (īṃ) (f. pl. **only used when the Pfct. part. is used without a form of 'to be' present**)	बोलीं (bolīṃ)

[1] In Hindi grammar the infinitive is called 'क्रिया का मूलरूप' (kriyā kā mūlrūp). The infinitive can be used as a noun: बोलना (bolnā): 'the act of speaking'. Such nouns follow the declension of m. nouns -ā (बेटा).

[2] One should be extremely careful with the use of the stem imperative. In Indian society, social hierarchy is still much more firmly in place than in the West. If due respect is not expressed, a careless speaker can inadvertently insult Hindi speakers who consider themselves higher in rank than the person who is addressing them. Hence, stem imperatives should only be used among people one is very close with (a mother to her child), or toward people who are clearly lower on the social ladder than they are themselves (elder male toward a [younger] female).

VI.3. COMPOUND VERBAL TENSES

VI.3.1. IMPERFECTIVE PRESENT (वर्तमान काल VARTAMĀN KĀL) AND PAST (अपूर्ण भूतकाल APŪRṆ BHŪTKĀL)

Imperfective present	=	present part.	+	present of होना (honā)
Imperfective past	=	present part.	+	past of होना (honā)

The present participle is used to indicate that an action is imperfect or incomplete. To indicate whether the incomplete action took place in the present or in the past, the present or past form of the verb होना (honā) is added to the present participle of the main verb. Hence, the present participle indicates that the action is incomplete; the present or past form of होना (honā) tells us whether the incomplete action takes place in the present or in the past.

The imperfective present is used to express habitual actions or general states. The imperfective past is used for habitual actions or habits, and general states in the past. Often, the imperfective verbs will be translated in English with 'used to'. The imperfective is not the appropriate tense to use for an action that occurred once in the past (see example below). One should use the perfective tense in such cases (see VI.3.2.).

Habitual present (imperfect present) वर्तमान काल (vartamān kāl)	I speak मैं बोलती हूँ (maiṃ boltī hūṃ)
Habitual past (imperfect past) अपूर्ण भूतकाल (apūrṇ bhūtkāl)	I spoke (I used to speak) मैं बोलती थी (maiṃ boltī thī)

Examples:

Every man makes mistakes, and I too made a mistake. (Varmā)

हर एक आदमी गलती करता है, मैंने भी ग़लती की। (har ek ādmī galtī kartā hai, maiṃne bhī galtī kī.)

In the morning, I drink tea.

सुबह में मैं चाय पीती हूँ। (subah meṃ maiṃ cāy pītī hūṃ.)

You will not believe me, but I tell the truth. (Yaśpāl)
तुम मानोगे नहीं लेकिन मैं सच कहता हूँ। (tum mānoge nahīṃ lekin maiṃ sac kahtā hūṃ.)

When I was little, I used to live in Delhi.
जब मैं छोटी थी तब मैं दिल्ली में रहती थी। (jab maiṃ choṭī thī tab maiṃ dillī meṃ rahtī thī.)

We buy a book every week.
हम हर हफ़्ते एक किताब ख़रीदते हैं। (ham har hafte ek kitāb kharīdte haiṃ.)

Table 20. Imperfective: Conjugation of example verb देखना (dekhnā) 'to see'

	MASCULINE		FEMININE	
	PRESENT	PAST	PRESENT	PAST
1 sg मैं (maiṃ)	देखता हूँ (dekhtā hūṃ)	देखता था (dekhtā thā)	देखती हूँ (dekhtī hūṃ)	देखती थी (dekhtī thī)
2 sg तू (tū)	देखता है (dekhtā hai)	देखता था (dekhtā thā)	देखती है (dekhtī hai)	देखती थी (dekhtī thī)
3 sg वह/यह (vah/yah)	देखता है (dekhtā hai)	देखता था (dekhtā thā)	देखती है (dekhtī hai)	देखती थी (dekhtī thī)
1 pl हम (ham)	देखते हैं (dekhte haiṃ)	देखते थे (dekhte the)	देखती हैं (dekhtī haiṃ)	देखती थीं (dekhtī thīṃ)
2 pl तुम (tum)	देखते हो (dekhte ho)	देखते थे (dekhte the)	देखती हो (dekhtī ho)	देखती थीं (dekhtī thīṃ)
3 pl वे/ये/आप (ve/ye/āp)	देखते हैं (dekhte haiṃ)	देखते थे (dekhte the)	देखती हैं (dekhtī haiṃ)	देखती थीं (dekhtī thīṃ)

VI.3.2. PERFECTIVE TENSE (पूर्ण काल PŪRṆ KĀL)

Contrary to the imperfective, describing habitual actions or conditions, the perfective is used to express actions that are completed and happened at a specific moment in time, e.g., "we used to go there every summer" would call for an imperfective, but "we went there twice" would be expressed in the perfective. Imperfective and perfective cannot be used interchangeably.

Simple past	=	past participle		
Present perfect	=	past participle	+	present of होना (honā)
Past perfect or more remote past	=	past participle	+	past of होना (honā)

Table 21. Perfective: Conjugation of example verb बोलना (bolnā) 'to speak'

	MASCULINE		FEMININE	
	PERFECT	PERFECT PRESENT/PAST	PERFECT	PERFECT PRESENT/PAST
1 sg मैं (maiṃ)	बोला (bolā)	बोला हूँ/था (bolā hūṃ/thā)	बोली (bolī)	बोली हूँ/थी (bolī hūṃ/thī)
2 sg तू (tū)	बोला (bolā)	बोला है/था (bolā hai/thā)	बोली (bolī)	बोली है/थी (bolī hai/thī)
3 sg वह/यह (vah/yah)	बोला (bolā)	बोला है/था (bolā hai/thā)	बोली (bolī)	बोली है/थी (bolī hai/thī)
1 pl हम (ham)	बोले (bole)	बोले हैं/थे (bole haiṃ/the)	बोलीं (bolīṃ)	बोली हैं/थीं (bolī haiṃ/thīṃ)
2 pl तुम (tum)	बोले (bole)	बोले हो/थे (bole ho/the)	बोलीं (bolīṃ)	बोली हो/थीं (bolī ho/thīṃ)
3 pl वे/ये/आप (ve/ye/āp)	बोले (bole)	बोले हैं/थे (bole haiṃ/the)	बोलीं (bolīṃ)	बोली हैं/थीं (bolī haiṃ/thīṃ)

Traditionally, English speakers consider using the perfective tenses in Hindi somewhat more challenging than other verbal tenses. This is because it is important to understand the difference between transitive and intransitive verbs. In the perfective tense, intransitive verbs will prove largely uncomplicated, with the Hindi and English subject remaining the same. However, transitive verbs in the perfective tense will use the (in English untranslatable) particle ने (ne) following the English or "logical" subject, which will impact the verb agreement (see VI.3.2.1.).

Intransitive verbs are verbs that do not take an object, e.g., to go, to come. One could state that there is no meaningful what or who question that can be asked using the subject and the verb. E.g., "The woman came here." > "The woman came what/who?" is not a meaningful question; hence there is no direct object in this sentence.

Conversely, transitive verbs require an object in order to make sense.[1] To find the direct object of a sentence, one can ask a what or who question about the sentence, using the subject and the verb of the sentence. E.g., "The boy is reading a book." > "The boy is reading what?" Here, 'a book' is the direct object.

The past or perfective participle is used either independently as the finite verb (simple past) or in compound forms (present perfect and past perfect) to indicate that the action has been completed. The difference between simple past, present perfect, and past perfect is the relationship of the action in the past to the present. The simple past has no specific connection to the present. The focus is not on the context, but solely on the completion of the action in the past. The present perfect is sometimes referred to as immediate past: it is generally used to describe actions that have been recently completed and have a clear connection to, or impact on, the present. The past perfect or (more) remote past is used to describe actions that are further in the past than other actions in the past. There is no immediate link with, or impact on, the present.

Simple past सामान्य भूतकाल (sāmāny bhūtkāl)	I spoke मैं बोली (maiṃ bolī)
Present perfect पूर्ण वर्तमाण काल (pūrṇ vartamān kāl)	I have spoken मैं बोलीहूँ (maiṃ bolī hūṃ)
Past perfect पूर्ण भूतकाल (pūrṇ bhūtkāl)	I had spoken मैं बोली थी (maiṃ bolī thī)

1. Note that all causative and double causative verbs are transitive.

Examples:

[Before my leaving] all family members had explained to me that pickpocketing is frequent in Delhi. (Yaśpāl) (*first action takes place further in the past than the story that is set in the past*)

[जाने से पहले] घर के लोगों ने समझाया था, दिल्ली में जेबकट बहुत हैं। ([jāne se pahle] ghar ke logoṃ ne samajhāyā thā, dillī meṃ jebkaṭ bahut haiṃ.)

My mother had always taught me: "Son, if ever someone offers you anything, do not take it."

माँ ने सदा यही सिखाया था - बेटा, कभी कोई कुछ दे तो भी नहीं लेना। (māṃ ne sadā yahī sikhāyā thā - beṭā, kabhī koī kuch de to bhī nahīṃ lenā.) (Yaśpāl)

Darling, look what gift I brought for you. (Gulzār) (*clear impact on the present*)

प्यारी, देखो मैं तुम्हारे लिए क्या तोहफ़ा लाया हूँ। (pyārī, dekho maiṃ tumhāre lie kyā tohfā lāyā hūṃ.)

At that moment, Ghīsū remembered that wedding party of the *ṭhākur* he had attended twenty years before. (Premcand)

घीसू को उस वक़्त ठाकुर की बारात याद आई जिसमें बीस साल पहले वह गया था। (ghīsū ko us vaqt ṭhākur kī bārāt yād āī jis meṃ bīs sāl pahle vah gayā thā.)

VI.3.2.1. THE ने (NE) CONSTRUCTION

When the main verb in the sentence is both perfective[2] and transitive[3] the subject is followed by the untranslatable grammatical postposition ने (ne). As a result, the subject is put into the oblique case. Because of the particle ने (ne), the verb cannot agree with the English or logical subject, and will agree with the direct object instead.

---

2. This means if the verb is put in the simple past, present perfect, past perfect, past potential, past presumptive, or past irrealis tense.
3. See VI.3.2. for an explanation of transitive verbs.

Example:

He came in (intransitive and perfective: no ने (ne) is used and the verb can agree with the subject) and drank tea (f.) (transitive and perfective: ने (ne) is used and thus the verb cannot agree with the subject and agrees with the object).

वह अन्दर आया और उसने चाय पी। (vah andar āyā aur usne cāy pī.)

Note: There are two kinds of direct objects. In Hindi grammar, a distinction is made between animate (constructed with को) and inanimate direct objects (constructed with or without को). (See I.2.3.1.2.)

VI.3.2.2. THE ने (NE) CONSTRUCTION WHEN THE DIRECT OBJECT DOES NOT TAKE को (KO)

When the ने (ne) construction is used and the direct object is indefinite and inanimate, indefinite and animate, or sometimes when definite and inanimate (i.e., when used without को (ko)),[4] the verb will agree with the direct object.

Examples:

Kallū (m.) took <u>the tea</u>. (Bismillāh)

कल्लू ने <u>चाय</u> ले ली। (kallū ne <u>cāy</u> le lī.)

Pahalvān (m.) had taken <u>an oath</u> at that time. (Rākeś)

पहलवान ने तब <u>क़सम</u> खाई थी। (pahalvān ne tab <u>qasm</u> khāī thī.)

Ṭinnū (m.) stopped drinking <u>tea</u>. (Bismillāh)

टिन्नू ने <u>चाय</u> पीनी बंद कर दी। (ṭinnū ne <u>cāy</u> pīnī band kar dī.)

VI.3.2.3. THE ने (NE) CONSTRUCTION WHEN THE DIRECT OBJECT DOES TAKE को (KO)

When the ने (ne) construction is used, and the sentence has a direct object that is definite and animate, or in some cases definite and

4. The direct object in the example sentences is underlined.

inanimate (i.e., constructed with को), the verb will be put in the neutral form, being the masculine singular.[5]

Examples:

I saw you people when I arrived. (Rākeś)
मैंने आकर तुम लोगों को देख लिया। (maiṃne ākar tum logoṃ ko dekh liyā.)

She woke Kallū by shaking him (i.e., she shook him awake). (Bismillāh)
उसने झकझोरकर कल्लू को जगाया। (usne jhakjhorkar kallū ko jagāyā.)

She had seen the girl.
उसने लड़की को देखा था। (usne laṛkī ko dekhā thā.)

The young man stopped rattling the bunch of keys and kept them in his fist. (Rākeś)
नवयुवक ने चाबियों के गुच्छे को हिलाना बन्द करके अपनी मुट्ठी में ले लिया। (navyuvak ne cābiyoṃ ke gucche ko hilānā band karke apnī muṭṭhī meṃ le liyā.)

Remark: In the sentences above, टिन्नू ने चाय पीनी बंद कर दी। (ṭinnū ne cāy pīnī band kar dī) and नवयुवक ने चाबियों के गुच्छे को हिलाना बन्द करके अपनी मुट्ठी में ले लिया। (navyuvak ne cābiyoṃ ke gucche ko hilānā band karke apnī muṭṭhī meṃ le liyā), the direct object contains a noun followed by an infinitive: चाय पीना (cāy pīnā) 'to drink tea' and चाबियों के गुच्छे को हिलाना (cābiyoṃ ke gucche ko hilānā) 'to rattle the bunch of keys'. When the actual subject of the sentence is followed by ने (ne), the direct object becomes the grammatical subject of the sentence. When the grammatical subject consists of a noun and an infinitive, the infinitive can agree in number and gender with the noun. 'Tea' is f., hence in the sentence above, the infinitive 'to drink' 'पीना' (pīnā) agrees with 'tea' and becomes पीनी (pīnī). However, when the noun is followed by को (ko), the infinitive cannot agree with the noun. In the example चाबियों के गुच्छे को (cābiyoṃ ke gucche ko), the infinitive हिलाना (hilānā) does not agree with 'keys', because of the को (ko).

5. The direct object in the example sentences is underlined.

VI.3.2.4. SOME SPECIAL TRANSITIVE VERBS THAT DO NOT TAKE ने (NE)

Notwithstanding the fact that they are transitive verbs, some verbs do not take ने (ne):[6]

बकना (baknā) 'to babble, to talk nonsense'[7]

बोलना (bolnā) 'to speak'[8]

Note: bolnā will take ने (ne) in combination with nouns: झूठ बोलना (jhūṭh bolnā) 'to tell a lie'

भूलना (bhūlnā) 'to forget'

लाना (lānā) 'to bring'

पढ़ना (paṛhnā) in the sense of 'to take a course (in history, writing)'

The following verbs are both transitive and intransitive:

लड़ना (laṛnā) 'to fight'

रोना (ronā) 'to cry'

मुसकराना (muskarānā) 'to smile'

When a cognate object (a tear, a smile) is expressed, constructions both with and without ने are possible.

E.g., He smiled the smile of victory.

वह विजय की मुसकराहट मुसकराया। (vah vijay kī muskarāhaṭ muskarāyā.)

उसने विजय की मुसकराहट मुसकराई। (usne vijay kī muskarāhaṭ muskarāī.)

समझना (samajhnā) 'to understand' is constructed both with and without ने.

E.g., Did you see/understand my point?

क्या आप मेरी बात समझे। (kyā āp merī bāt samajhe.)

क्या आपने मेरी बात समझी। (kyā āp ne merī bāt samajhī.)

Notice that the following verbs are intransitive and never take ने, not even if there is a cognate object present:

---

6. McGregor, *Outline of Hindi*, 78–82.
7. In some dictionaries, this verb is listed as intransitive (e.g., McGregor, *The Oxford Hindi-English Dictionary*).
8. In some dictionaries, this verb is listed as intransitive.

सोना (sonā) 'to sleep'
हँसना (haṃsnā) 'to laugh'
E.g., He slept the sleep of the just.
वह बेफ़िक्री की नींद सोया। (vah befiqrī kī nīṃd soyā.)

VI.3.2.5. SPECIAL INTRANSITIVE VERBS THAT DO TAKE ने (NE)

The following verb is actually intransitive, but can be constructed with ने (ne):

नहाना (nahānā) 'to bathe' is constructed both with or without ने (ne).

The following two verbs are intransitive, but always take ने (ne). As a result, the verb is always constructed in the m. sg.

खाँसना (khāṃsnā) 'to cough'
छींकना (chīṃknā) 'to sneeze'

Notes:

1. Some verbs are not transitive in English but are in Hindi, and vice versa. This is specifically the case with verbs that consist of a noun or adjective and the verb करना (karnā), e.g., इंतज़ार करना (intazār karnā) 'to wait'.

Examples:

I have waited for you.
मैंने आपका इन्तज़ार किया। (maiṃne āpkā intazar kiyā.)

The old man tried [to smile]. (Rākeś)
बुड्ढे ने [मुसकराने की] कोशिश की। (buḍḍhe ne [muskarāne kī] kośiś kī.)

2. Sometimes, the main verb might be transitive, but in fixed combinations, the ने (ne) will not be used: दिखाई देना (dikhāī denā) 'to be visible' and सुनाई देना (sunāī denā) 'to be audible' are both intransitive, notwithstanding the fact that देना (denā) is transitive.

Examples:

A heavy-looking shining object became visible. (Bismillāh)
भारी-सी चीज़ चमकती हुई दिखाई दी। (bhārī-sī cīz camaktī huī dikhāī dī.)

Suddenly, a song became audible.
अचानक एक गीत सुनाई दिया। (acānak ek gīt sunāī diyā.)

VI.3.2.6. AUXILIARY VERBS AND THE USAGE OF ने (NE)

Whenever a verb is used in combination with an auxiliary or vector verb (see VII.), the use or absence of ने (ne) can be determined by the transitive or intransitive character of the auxiliary verb, and not necessarily by that of the main verb.

A. Auxiliary verbs that do not take ने (ne)

आना (ānā)
उठना (uṭhnā)
करना (karnā)
जाना (jānā)
पड़ना (paṛnā)
पाना (pānā)
बैठना (baiṭhnā)
रहना (rahnā)
लगना (lagnā)
सकना (saknā)

B. Auxiliary verbs that do take ने (ne)

चाहना (cāhnā)
चुकना (cuknā)
डालना (ḍālnā)
देना (denā) (in rare cases, ने (ne) is not used when the main verb is intransitive; see VII.8.)
रखना (rakhnā)
लेना (lenā)

VI.3.3 CONTINUOUS TENSE (अपूर्ण काल APŪRṆ KĀL)

Continuous present	=	stem	+	past part. of रहना (rahnā)	+	present of होना (honā)
Continuous past	=	stem	+	past part. of रहना (rahnā)	+	past of होना (honā)

The continuous tense expresses the fact that the action is in progress. The aspect of the ongoing character is stressed in the continuous tense, contrary to the imperfective tense, which merely describes a habit or condition. The continuous tense is formed by combining the stem of the main verb with the past participle[9] of the verb रहना (rahnā) 'to stay' and the present or past tense of the verb होना (honā) 'to be'. The ongoing action can be situated in the past or in the present. In English, this tense is often translated with the '-ing' form of the main verb.

Continuous present
सतत्य वर्तमान (sataty vartamān)

I am talking
मैं बोल रही हूँ (maiṃ bol rahī hūṃ.)

Continuous past
सतत्य भूतकाल (sataty bhūtkāl)

I was talking
मैं बोल रही थी (maiṃ bol rahī thī.)

Examples:

What are you (m.) doing? I am watching a film.
तुम क्या कर रहे हो? मैं चलचित्र देख रही हूँ। (tum kyā kar rahe ho? maiṃ calcitr dekh rahī hūṃ.)

A faqīr was playing the iktārā and singing something. (Yaśpāl)
एक फकीर इकतारा बजा कर कुछ गा रहा था। (ek faqīr iktārā bajā kar kuch gā rahā thā.)

He was talking, everybody was listening. (Bismillāh)
वह बोल रहे थे, सब सुन रहे थे। (vah bol rahe the, sab sun rahe the.)

9. Both in the present and in the past continuous, the past participle is used, never the present participle. Note that in this compound verbal construction, the past participle does not indicate that the action is past or completed.

I was eating when he came in.

जब वह अन्दर आया तब मैं खा रही थी। (jab vah andar āyā tab maiṃ khā rahī thī.)

Table 22. Continuous: Conjugation of example verb देखना (dekhnā) 'to see'

	MASCULINE		FEMININE	
	PRESENT	PAST	PRESENT	PAST
1 sg मैं (maiṃ)	देख रहा हूँ (dekh rahā hūṃ)	देख रहा था (dekh rahā thā)	देख रही हूँ (dekh rahī hūṃ)	देख रही थी (dekh rahī thī)
2 sg तू (tū)	देख रहा है (dekh rahā hai)	देख रहा था (dekh rahā thā)	देख रही है (dekh rahī hai)	देख रही थी (dekh rahī thī)
3 sg वह/यह (vah/yah)	देख रहा है (dekh rahā hai)	देख रहा था (dekh rahā thā)	देख रही है (dekh rahī hai)	देख रही थी (dekh rahī thī)
1 pl हम (ham)	देख रहे हैं (dekh rahe haiṃ)	देख रहे थे (dekh rahe the)	देख रही हैं (dekh rahī haiṃ)	देख रही थीं (dekh rahī thīṃ)
2 pl तुम (tum)	देख रहे हो (dekh rahe ho)	देख रहे थे (dekh rahe the)	देख रही हो (dekh rahī ho)	देख रही थीं (dekh rahī thīṃ)
3 pl वे/ये/आप (ve/ye/āp)	देख रहे हैं (dekh rahe haiṃ)	देख रहे थे (dekh rahe the)	देख रही हैं (dekh rahī haiṃ)	देख रही थीं (dekh rahī thīṃ)

VI.3.4. UNFULFILLABLE/UNFULFILLED CONDITIONS: IRREALIS

Imperfect irrealis	=	present part.	+	present part. of होना (honā)
Past irrealis	=	past part.	+	present part. of होना (honā)
Continuous irrealis	=	continuous	+	present part. of होना (honā)

The combination of a present participle, past participle, or continuous with a present participle of होना (honā) is called the irrealis. This form implies that a condition is either unfulfillable or will stay unfulfilled. Note that past irrealis of transitive verbs requires ने (ne).

This specific combination of verbs can be replaced by the usage of an independent present participle, which often is the case in spoken Hindi (see VI.4.5.).

Imperfect irrealis	if I (m.) would speak मैं बोलता होता (maiṃ boltā hotā)
Past irrealis	if I (f.) had spoken मैं बोली होती (maiṃ bolī hotī)
Continuous irrealis	if I (m.) were speaking मैं बोल रहा होता (maiṃ bol rahā hotā)

Examples:

[Luckily] his sister grabbed him just in time; if not, that man would surely have taken him along. (but this did not happen) (Rākeś)

उसकी बहन वक़्त पर उसे पकड़ लाई, नहीं तो वह आदमी उसे ले गया होता। (uskī bahan vaqt par use pakaṛ lāī, nahīṃ to vah ādmī use le gayā hotā.)

If I had gone home, this would never have happened.

अगर मैं घर गया होता तो यह कभी नहीं हुआ होता। (agar maiṃ ghar gayā hotā to yah kabhī nahīṃ huā hotā.)

If I had read that book, I would have known.

अगर मैंने यह किताब पढ़ी होती तो मुझे मालूम होता। (agar maiṃ yah kitāb paṛhī hotī to mujhe mālūm hotā.)

Note that one can always add a thought ("but I did not go home," "but I do not live there," "but I did not read that book") and, as a consequence, the condition is unfulfilled and the sentence is not real, the action did not take place, the situation never occurred/will never occur.

VI.3.5. CONDITIONAL OR POTENTIAL (हेतुहेतुमत काल HETUHETUMAT KĀL)

Imperfect conditional	=	present part.	+	subjunctive of होना (honā)
Past conditional	=	past part.	+	subjunctive of होना (honā)
Continuous conditional	=	continuous	+	subjunctive of होना (honā)

The present participle, past participle, or continuous can also be combined with a subjunctive of होना (honā). This combination forms the imperfect, past, and continuous conditional tense, respectively. The subjunctive indicates that there is an uncertainty or even unlikeliness that the action will take place. The action is not impossible but will only occur if certain requirements are met. Note that the past conditional of transitive verbs requires ने (ne).

This specific combination of verbs can be replaced by the usage of the subjunctive or imperfective in the conditional clause, if the result is possible or probable to happen, but has not been confirmed. The perfect tense can be used in the conditional clause, to indicate that the result would be guaranteed, if the condition in the clause were to be fulfilled. The clause of the sentence that presents the result or consequence can be in the future, present, or imperative.

Imperfect conditional	If I (f.) would speak (I could speak) मैं बोलती होऊँ (maiṃ boltī hoūṃ)
Past conditional	If I (f.) would have spoken (I could have spoken) मैं बोली होऊँ (maiṃ bolī hoūṃ)
Continuous conditional	If I (f.) would be speaking (I could have been speaking) मैं बोल रही होऊँ (maiṃ bol rahī hoūṃ)

Examples:

If you would be sleeping, I could work.

अगर तुम सो रहे हो तो मैं काम कर सकूँ। (agar tum so rahe ho to maiṃ kām kar sakūṃ.)

If she would come to Lahore [regularly], she could meet us there.

अगर वह लाहोर को आती होवे तो वह हम से वहाँ मिल सके। (agar vah lāhor ko ātī hove to vah ham se vahāṃ mil sake.)

[If he] would come into [my] possession, I could swallow him in one gulp! (*a crocodile dreaming about eating a monkey*) (Gulzār)

हाथ लग जाए तो एक ही घूँठ में सुड़क जाऊँ। (hāth lag jāe to ek hī ghūṃṭh meṃ suṛak jāūṃ.)

Examples in which the conditional has been replaced by the perfect tense:

If you gave money to that family, they would be able to buy medication. (*indicating that the subject has made clear he will not give money*)

अगर आप ने उस परिवार को पैसे दिये तो वे दवाई ख़रीद सकते हैं। (agar āp ne us parivār ko paise diye to ve davāī kharīd sakte haiṃ.)

If I finish this today, I will (be able to) relax for a month. (*setting a benchmark*)

अगर आज मैं ने उसे ख़त्म किया तो महीने के लिए आराम करूँगी (agar āj maiṃ ne use khatm kiyā to mahīne ke lie ārām karūṃgī.)

VI.3.6. PRESUMPTIVE (संदिग्ध काल SANDIGDH KĀL)

Imperfect presumptive	=	present part.	+	future of होना (honā)
Past presumptive	=	past part.	+	future of होना (honā)
Continuous presumptive	=	continuous	+	future of होना (honā)

The presumptive (अनुमान बोधक वाक्य-रचना anumān bodhak vāky-racnā) is used more frequently in Hindi than the irrealis and conditional. One can also come across the combination of a present participle, past participle, or continuous with the future tense of होना (honā). This forms the imperfect, perfect, and continuous presumptive tense respectively. The presumptive can be used to make statements based on a presumption. Note that past presumptive of transitive verbs requires ने (ne).

Imperfect presumptive — He will probably (must) speak
वह बोलता होगा (vah boltā hogā)

Past presumptive — I must have spoken
मैं बोली हूँगी (maiṃ bolī hūṃgī)

Continuous presumptive — She must be speaking
वह बोल रही होगी (vah bol rahī hogī)

Examples:

Hurry up, friend, my wife must be at home worrying. (Gulzār)

जल्दी करना दोस्त, घर पर मेरी पत्नी बेचैन हो रही होगी। (jaldī karnā dost, ghar par merī patnī becain ho rahī hogī.)

Her age must have been around thirty. (Varmā)

उसकी अवस्था[10] लगभग तीस वर्ष की रही होगी। (uskī avasthā lagbhag tīs varṣ kī rahī hogī.)

The one who eats such sweet fruit daily must have a very sweet heart. (*a crocodile dreaming out loud about how tasty his prey will be*) (Gulzār)

ऐसा मीठा फल जो रोज़ खाता होगा, उसका दिल कितना मीठा होगा। (aisā mīṭhā phal jo roz khātā hogā, uskā dil kitnā mīṭhā hogā.)

You must have eaten about twenty pūrīs. (Premcand)

तुमने एक बीस पूरियाँ खाई होंगी। (tumne ek bīs pūriyāṃ khāī hoṃgī.)

VI.4. SIMPLE VERBAL TENSES

Apart from the compound verbal tenses, there are also five simple verbal tenses that do not take a form of होना (honā): absolutive, imperative, subjunctive, future, and present participle used independently.

VI.4.1. ABSOLUTIVE (पूर्वकालिक कृदंत PŪRVAKĀLIK KṚDANT)

Absolutive	=	stem	+	- ∅
	=	stem	+	-कर (-kar)
	=	stem	+	-के (-ke)

The absolutive or conjunctive participle is used to express that two actions happen in a sequence, or sometimes simultaneously.[11] The verb in the absolutive can be translated as happening prior to the action expressed by the conjugated verb of the sentence. One can often use 'after…-ing' in translation, e.g., वह दरवाज़ा खोलकर अन्दर आया (vah

10. अवस्था (avasthā), uncommon and poetic word used for उम्र (umr) 'age'.
11. McGregor, *Outline of Hindi*, 42.

darvāzā kholkar andar āyā) 'After opening the door, he came inside' or 'He opened the door and came inside'.

While the absolutive can be used in an adverbial way, to express the way in which the main verb happened (e.g., वह घबरा कर बोला (vah ghabrā kar bolā) 'he spoke anxiously', i.e., he spoke while being anxious),[12] some caution must be exercised regarding such use of the absolutive. Many verbs expressing an action can only be used in the absolutive to express the sequential occurrence of two actions and not their simultaneity. Note that Usha Jain lists only two "exceptional examples" where the absolutive is translated with an adverb, and does not mention the use of absolutive to express actions that happen simultaneously: सम्भालकर (sambhālkar) 'carefully' and मेहरबानी करके (meharbānī karke) 'kindly'.[13] Surely मिलकर (milkar) 'unitedly, together', and घबराकर (ghabrākar) 'perplexed, anxiously' could be added to these.

When discussing the limitations of translating absolutives simultaneously with the action of the main verb, native speakers seemed to agree that few absolutives of verbs can be translated thus, the reasoning being that in a sentence like वह दरवाज़ा खोलकर अन्दर आया (vah darvāzā kholkar andar āyā) 'He opened the door and came in', the absolutive would be seen as a verb that was a condition for the main verb to take place: in order to go inside, the door needs to be opened. However, in a sentence such as वह रोकर अन्दर आया (vah rokar andar āyā) 'He cried and came in', the absolutive would indicate that the subject finished crying, and then came inside; translating 'rokar' adverbially/simultaneously as 'while crying/cryingly' would be considered inaccurate. Native speakers generally agree that the use of absolutive to express simultaneous actions has to be restricted; when the absolutive describes the fashion in which the main action occurs (e.g., 'she entered while crying'), the participle used adverbially will be used rather than the absolutive (see VIII.4.).

However, it must be noted that skilled writers like Premcand[14]

12. The absolutive is described to be used in this way by many grammarians. See McGregor, *Outline of Hindi*, 42. Example taken from Schmidt, *Essential Urdu*, 186.
13. Jain, *Introduction to Hindi*, 247–248.
14. Schmidt lists an example taken from Godān: "bātēṃ to haṃs haṃs kē kar rahē thē": "He was talking cheerfully (having smiled-smiled)" (Schmidt, *Essential Urdu*, 186).

did use the absolutive in a way that could be seen as expressing simultaneity. In such cases, absolutives are used adverbially. This leaves the impression that the use of the absolutive might be changing, and now is being used almost exclusively to express succession and less to express simultaneity, for which participles seem to be preferred.

Absolutive	'speaking' or 'having spoken' बोलकर or बोलके (bolkar / bolke)[15]

Note: The endings -करके (karke) and -करकर (karkar) (e.g., बोलकरके (bolkarke) and बोलकरकर (bolkarkar)) are only used in colloquial speech.

Examples:

Shaśibālādevī giggled and burst into laughter. (Varmā)

शशिबालादेवी खिलखिलाकर हँस पड़ीं।[16] (śaśibālādevī khilkhilākar hāṃs paṛīṃ.)

Then he put his slippers on his feet and went outside. (Bismillāh)

फिर पाँवों में चप्पल डालकर बाहर निकल गया। (phir pāṃvoṃ meṃ cappal ḍālkar bāhar nikal gayā.)

Mādhav looked at the sky and spoke [...] (Premcand)

माधव आसमान की तरफ़ देखकर बोला [...] (mādhav āsmān kī taraf dekhkar bolā [...])

VI.4.2. IMPERATIVE (विधिकाल VIDHIKĀL)

Stem imperative	=	stem	+	- Ø
Informal imperative	=	stem	+	-ओ (-o)
Formal/honorific imperative	=	stem	+	-इए (-ie)
	=	stem	+	-इएगा (-iegā)
General imperative	=	stem	+	-ना (-nā)

15. Note that there is no difference in meaning between both forms. Both can be translated simultaneously or consecutively.
16. The feminine plural form is used here to express respect toward a female of high rank.

Contrary to other verbal forms, imperatives do not reflect the gender or number of the doer of the action. However, there are different kinds of imperatives, reflecting social hierarchy, and hence indicating the degree of formality between the speaker and the subject.

The stem imperative should be used with caution. It can imply contempt from the speaker for the addressee. Often, this form can be heard when a superior is addressing servants or people they consider to be their subordinate or even inferior, like beggars. The same form is used when talking to pets or animals. People who are very close or intimate (lovers, a mother to her child) can also use this form; that is to say, the 'superior' will use it when ordering a subordinate. Be careful when using this form of imperative. Do not use it frivolously. Another application of this form can be commonly found in (Sufi) poetry or songs, when the poet is addressing God.

The imperative ending in -ओ (-o) is called the informal imperative. It can be used when addressing social and hierarchical equals or subordinates, never to superiors (a teacher to a student, sisters or brothers among themselves, friends, parents to children, etc.). Some verbs have an irregular informal imperative (see VI.6.). It is important to note that in modern times, this imperative is used increasingly without a connotation of feeling of superiority of the speaker. It is used to express urgency, implying that the order should be conducted without delay. This can be seen in contrast with the infinitive used as imperative. For example, a mother is going out for the evening and says to her daughter, रात में दरवाजा बन्द करो! (rāt meṃ dārvāzā band karo!) 'Close the door at night!' This can be seen as a direct order to lock the door in this specific instance. By contrast, consider the situation that a daughter is going to study and is moving to campus. Before her departure, the mother says, रात में दरवाजा बन्द करना! (rāt meṃ dārvāzā band karnā!) 'Close the door at night!' Here, the infinitive is used to give the daughter advice, a reminder of something they both know she already knows, rather than a specific order.

Imperatives ending in -इए (-ie) are called honorific or formal imperatives. This form can be used to address superiors, elderly, strangers of whom one is unsure about their rank. This imperative expresses respect. The alternative ending -इएगा (-iegā) (invariably ending in -ā) is even more formal/polite. For some verbs, this form is irregular (see VI.6.). Alternatively, the subjunctive 3 pl. can be used as well (see VI.4.3.).

Note that if the formal imperative is used between people with an informal relationship, this imperative can be used sarcastically, for example, if repeated requests between friends to return a borrowed item using a less formal imperative have not generated the desired result, one can repeat the request in the formal imperative.

The infinitive used as an imperative is called the general imperative. This form is more polite than the informal, but less polite than the honorific imperative. It is often used to address a group, to give general instructions or advice (see supra under imperative ending in -o).

Examples:

[an old man to a child]: "I (*pl. used for respect*) will give you something, come!" (Rākeś)

तुझे चिज्जी देंगे, आ। (tujhe cizzī deṃge, ā!)

[a man to bystanders, with urgency]: "Oh, somebody, save me!" (Rākeś)

हाय, कोई मुझे बचाओ! (hāy, koī mujhe bacāo!)

[a military to a lower in rank]: "Send him (*pl. used for respect*) to that post immediately!" (Bismillāh)

इन्हें फ़ौरन उस पोस्ट पर भेजो। (inheṃ fauran us posṭ par bhejo!)

[a man to a man that is the same age, but socially a superior]: "Please, drink the tea!" (Bismillāh)

चाय पीजिए! (cāy pījie!)

[a bystander to an older man]: "I beg your pardon, Mr. Siddīqī, but there is one thing I would like to know." (Bismillāh)

माफ़ कीजिएगा सिद्दीक़ी साहब, मैं एक बात जानना चाहता हूँ। (māf kījiegā siddīqī sāhab, maiṃ ek bāt jānnā cāhtā hūṃ.)

[an old woman to a younger man]:[17] "First listen and then talk to me." (Ugra)

पहले मेरी बातें सुन लो फिर मुझसे कुछ कहना। (pahle merī bātem̩ sun lo phir mujhse kuch kahnā.)

The negation of the imperative is done in two different ways. The stem imperative and informal imperatives are negated with मत (mat). The formal imperative takes the negation particle न (na). However, in colloquial Hindi, often मत (mat) is used here. The infinitive can be both negated with मत (mat) and न (na).

Examples:

Don't think I never had the desire to marry! (Varmā)

आप यह न समझिएगा कि मेरी विवाह करने की कभी इच्छा ही न थी। (āp yah na samajhiegā ki merī vivāh karne kī icchā hī na thī!)

Don't send me a letter!

मुझे पत्र मत भेजो। (mujhe patr mat bhejo!)

Be quiet! Don't talk back! (*a teacher talking to students about proper behavior*)

चुप करना! उलटा जवाब मत/न देना! (cup karnā! ultā javāb mat/na denā!)

VI.4.3. SUBJUNCTIVE (संभावनार्थ SAṂBHĀVNĀRTH)

Subjunctive 1 sg. m./f.	=	stem	+	-ऊँ (-ūṃ)
Subjunctive 2 sg. m./f.	=	stem	+	-ए (-e)
Subjunctive 3 sg. m./f.	=	stem	+	-ए (-e)
Subjunctive 1 pl. m./f.	=	stem	+	-एँ (-eṃ)
Subjunctive 2 pl. m./f.	=	stem	+	-ओ (-o)
Subjunctive 3 pl. m./f.	=	stem	+	-एँ (-eṃ)

17. The age of the woman would make her a superior, but traditionally gender trumped age in social hierarchy. The general imperative can be seen as a compromise: she shows the young man greater respect than she would show a younger woman, yet she holds on to a certain level of superiority by not using the honorific imperative.

Note: There is no distinction between m. and f. forms in the subjunctive. The subjunctive is used for different purposes. It can express:

- a possibility
- a wish
- a hypothesis
- doubt (or a degree of uncertainty)
- a polite request
- an indirect order
- a suggestion or encouragement
- a request, asking for permission or advice
- a wish related to a third person ('Long live . . .')
- a hypothetical comparison ('he sat there as if he were waiting for someone'), often constructed with जैसे (jaise).

Table 23. Subjunctive of stem ending in a vowel: Example verb जाना (jānā) 'to go'

	MASCULINE FORM		FEMININE FORM	
1 sg मैं (maiṃ)	जाऊँ (jāūṃ)	I should go	जाऊँ (jāūṃ)	I should go
2 sg तू (tū)	जाए (jāe)	You should go	जाए (jāe)	You should go
3 sg वह/यह (vah/yah)	जाए (jāe)	He should go	जाए (jāe)	She should go
1 pl हम (ham)	जाएँ (jāeṃ)	We should go	जाएँ (jāeṃ)	We should go
2 pl तुम (tum)	जाओ (jāo)	You should go	जाओ (jāo)	You should go
3 pl वे/ये/आप (ve/ye/āp)	जाएँ (jāeṃ)	They/you should go	जाएँ (jāeṃ)	They/you should go

Table 24. Subjunctive of stem ending in a consonant: Example verb बोलना (bolnā) 'to speak'

	MASCULINE FORM		FEMININE FORM	
1 sg मैं (maiṃ)	बोलूँ (bolūṃ)	I should talk	बोलूँ (bolūṃ)	I should talk
2 sg तू (tū)	बोले (bole)	You should talk	बोले (bole)	You should talk
3 sg वह/यह (vah/yah)	बोले (bole)	He should talk	बोले (bole)	She should talk
1 pl हम (ham)	बोलें (boleṃ)	We should talk	बोलें (boleṃ)	We should talk
2 pl तुम (tum)	बोलो (bolo)	You should talk	बोलो (bolo)	You should talk
3 pl वे/ये/आप (ve/ye/āp)	बोलें (boleṃ)	They/you should talk	बोलें (boleṃ)	They/you should talk

When it is unsure or unlikely that a certain action will take place in the future, a subjunctive can be used instead of a future tense. The negation of subjunctive is not made with नहीं (nahīṃ), but with न (na).

The subjunctive is often used when making a polite request in more formal situations, in writing that includes directions (recipes, driving directions), or in official announcements and on public signs. E.g., कृपया आपकी कुर्सी की पेटी बाँधें। (kṛpayā āpkī kursī kī peṭī bāṃdheṃ) 'Please fasten your seatbelt'; कृपया धूम्रपान न करें। (kṛpayā dhūmrapān na kareṃ) 'No smoking, please'.

Examples:

[*a young man speaking to Gandhi*] Please stay right here. (Ugra)

आप यहीं रहें! (āp yahīṃ raheṃ.)

May God keep in mind the virtuous deeds of the good people and forgive the sins of the bad ones. (Rākeś)

खुदा नेक की नेकी बनाए रखे और बद् की बदी माफ़ करे। (khudā nek kī nekī banāe rakhe aur bad kī badī māf kare.)

What should I do now? (Gulzār)
अब क्या करूँ? (ab kyā karūṃ?)

Their eyes were glancing at everything as if that city were not an ordinary city, but a center of special attractiveness. (Rākeś)
उनकी आँखें वहाँ की हर चीज़ को देख रही थीं जैसे वह शहर साधारण शहर न होकर एक अच्छा-खासा आकर्षण-केन्द्र हो। (unkī āṃkheṃ vahāṃ kī har cīz ko dekh rahī thīṃ jaise vah śahr sādhāraṇ śahr na hokar ek acchā-khāsā ākarṣaṇ-kendra ho.)

[Do you think that] I would eat apples? Am I a vegetarian then? (*a crocodile being angry at her husband for bringing her apples*) (Gulzār)
मैं सेब खाऊँ? क्या मैं शाकाहारी हूँ? (maiṃ seb khāūṃ? kyā maiṃ śākāhārī hūṃ?)

Have you ever heard of the fact that there would be more than one heart in any being's chest? (Gulzār)
कभी सुना है किसी प्राणी के सीने में एक से ज़्यादा दिल हों? (kabhī sunā hai kisī prāṇī ke sīne meṃ ek se zyādā dil hoṃ?)

Following the words शायद (śāyad) 'maybe' and अगर (agar) 'if', the subjunctive is often used. When the following words are used in the main clause, the subjunctive will be used in the subordinate clause, i.e., the verb following the कि (ki), not the one preceding कि (ki).

'possible (that)'	सम्भव (sambhav),[18] मुमकिन (mumkin), हो सकता है (ho saktā hai)
'necessary (that)'	चाहिए कि (cāhie ki), ज़रूरी (zarūrī), अवश्यक (avaśyak)
'proper, suitable (that)'	मुनासिब (munāsib), उचित (ucit).

Examples:

It is possible that a cussing-match would erupt between them as well. (Rākeś)
हो सकता है दोनों में गाली-गलौज भी हो। (ho saktā hai donoṃ meṃ gālī-galauj bhī ho.)

18. When सम्भव (sambhav) is used in the sense of 'probable' and not 'possible', the verb following कि (ki) will not be put in the subjunctive. The meaning of the word is to be derived from the context.

Maybe he has forgotten about it.

शायद् वह भूल जाए। (śāyad vah bhūl jāe.)

It is possible that you would get angry as well when you come to know. (Varmā)

सम्भव है इसे जानकर तुम नाराज़ भी हो जाओ। (sambhav hai use jānkar tum nārāz bhī ho jāo.)

It will be proper that you go on your own.

मुनासिब होगा कि तुम अकेले जाओ। (munāsib hogā ki tum akele jāo.)

If you were not in a hurry, I could tell you [a story]. (Varmā)

अगर आप लोगों को कोई जल्दी न हो तो सुनाऊँ। (agar āp logoṃ ko koī jaldī na ho to sunāūṃ.)

VI.4.4. THE FUTURE (भविष्यत काल BHĀVIṢYAT KĀL)

Future 1 sg. m./f.	=	stem	+	-ऊँगा (-ūṃgā)/-ऊँगी (-ūṃgī)
Future 2 sg. m./f.	=	stem	+	-एगा (-egā)/-एगी (-egī)
Future 3 sg. m./f.	=	stem	+	-एगा (-egā)/-एगी (-egī)
Future 1 pl. m./f.	=	stem	+	-एँगे (-eṃge)/-एँगी (-eṃgī)
Future 2 pl. m./f.	=	stem	+	-ओगे (-oge)/-ओगी (-ogī)
Future 3 pl. m./f.	=	stem	+	-एँगे (-eṃge)/-एँगी (-eṃgī)

The future tense is used for actions that will take place in the future. To form the future tense, the ending -गा (-gā) for m. sg., -गे (-ge) for m. pl. is added to the subjunctive. For f. forms, both sg. and pl., -गी (-gī) is added. Hence, the gender of the verbal form can be deduced from the future ending, but the number is expressed in the subjunctive ending and not the future ending for the feminine forms.

Examples:

So I will come tomorrow at five in the evening. (Varmā)

तो कल शाम को पाँच बजे मैं आऊँगा। (to kal śām ko pāṃc baje maiṃ āūṃgā.)

What will people say when they will hear [this]? (Ugra)

लोग सुनेंगे तो क्या कहेंगे? (log suneṃge to kyā kaheṃge?)

Try one! [If] you will eat one, you will ask for more! (Gulzār)

एक खाके देखो। एक खाओगी तो और माँगोगी। (ek khāke dekho. ek khāogī to aur māṃgogī.)

Table 25. Future of stem ending in a vowel: Example verb जाना (jānā) 'to go'

	MASCULINE FORM		FEMININE FORM	
1 sg मैं (maiṃ)	जाऊँगा (jāūṃgā)	I will go	जाऊँगी (jāūṃgī)	I will go
2 sg तू (tū)	जाएगा (jāegā)	You will go	जाएगी (jāegī)	You will go
3 sg वह/यह (vah/yah)	जाएगा (jāegā)	He will go	जाएगी (jāegī)	She will go
1 pl हम (ham)	जाएँगे (jāeṃge)	We will go	जाएँगी (jāeṃgī)	We will go
2 pl तुम (tum)	जाओगे (jāoge)	You will go	जाओगी (jāogī)	You will go
3 pl वे/ये/आप (ve/ye/āp)	जाएँगे (jāeṃge)	They/you will go	जाएँगी (jāeṃgī)	They/you will go

Table 26. Future of stem ending in a consonant: Example verb बोलना (bolnā) 'to speak'

	MASCULINE FORM		FEMININE FORM	
1 sg मैं (maiṃ)	बोलूँगा (bolūṃgā)	I will talk	बोलूँगी (bolūṃgī)	I will talk
2 sg तू (tū)	बोलेगा (bolegā)	You will talk	बोलेगी (bolegī)	You will talk
3 sg वह/यह (vah/yah)	बोलेगा (bolegā)	He will talk	बोलेगी (bolegī)	She will talk
1 pl हम (ham)	बोलेंगे (boleṃge)	We will talk	बोलेंगी (boleṃgī)	We will talk
2 pl तुम (tum)	बोलोगे (bologe)	You will talk	बोलोगी (bologī)	You will talk
3 pl वे/ये/आप (ve/ye/āp)	बोलेंगे (boleṃge)	They/you will talk	बोलेंगी (boleṃgī)	They/you will talk

Table 27. Future of होना (honā) 'to be': Long form

	MASCULINE FORM		FEMININE FORM	
1 sg मैं (maiṃ)	होऊँगा (hoūṃgā)	I will be	होऊँगी (hoūṃgī)	I will be
2 sg तू (tū)	होएगा (hoegā)	You will be	होएगी (hoegī)	You will be
3 sg वह/यह (vah/yah)	होएगा (hoegā)	He will be	होएगी (hoegī)	She will be
1 pl हम (ham)	होएँगे (hoeṃge)	We will be	होएँगी (hoeṃgī)	We will be
2 pl तुम (tum)	होओगे (hooge)	You will be	होओगी (hoogī)	You will be
3 pl वे/ये/आप (ve/ye/āp)	होएँगे (hoeṃge)	They/you will be	होएँगी (hoeṃgī)	They/you will be

However, in the case of the verb 'to be', many forms also have an alternative shorter form.

Table 28. Future of होना (honā) 'to be': Common/short form

	MASCULINE FORM		FEMININE FORM	
1 sg मैं (maiṃ)	हूँगा (hūṃgā)	I will be	हूँगी (hūṃgī)	I will be
2 sg तू (tū)	होगा (hogā)	You will be	होगी (hogī)	You will be
3 sg वह/यह (vah/yah)	होगा (hogā)	He will be	होगी (hogī)	She will be
1 pl हम (ham)	होंगे (hoṃge)	We will be	होंगी (hoṃgī)	We will be
2 pl तुम (tum)	होगे (hoge)	You will be	होगी (hogī)	You will be
3 pl वे/ये/आप (ve/ye/āp)	होंगे (hoṃge)	They/you will be	होंगी (hoṃgī)	They/you will be

VI.4.5. PRESENT PARTICIPLE OR PAST PARTICIPLE USED AS FINITE VERB (कृदंत KṚDANT)

The present participle (भूतकालिक कृदंत bhūtkālik kṛdant) can be used independently. This can indicate a habit (in the past), an irrealis, an improbability in the future, or a conditional tense.

Note: When a sentence in the imperfective contains a negation, the conjugated form of होना (honā) can be dropped. Because of this, it looks as if the present participle is being used independently. This is not the case, however, and the usages should not be confused.

Examples:

Time and again I returned to the station. (Yaśpāl)
स्टेशन के समीप बार-बार जाता। (sṭeśan ke samīp bār-bār jātā.)

Why don't I do this [as a habit]? Listen! (Yaśpāl)
मैं ऐसा नहीं करता क्यों? सुनो! (maiṃ aisā nahīṃ kartā kyoṃ? suno!)

[Every time] he ate the apples and sat up until late, gossiping with Lālū. (Gulzār)
सेब खाता और देर तक वहीं बैठा लालू के साथ गपशप करता। (seb khātā aur der tak vahīṃ baiṭhā lālū ke sāth gapśap kartā.)

Whenever my son asked me full of love, "Mama, where is my dad?" I replied, "Poor boy, your dad has gone to heaven right before your birth." (Ugra)

मेरा बच्चा जब कभी मुझसे प्यार से पूछता कि 'माँ, मेरे अब्बा, कहाँ हैं?' तब मैं उत्तर देती कि 'अभागे तेरी पैदाइश के पहले ही तेरे अब्बा बहिश्त की ओर चले गए'। (merā baccā jab kabhī mujhse pyār se pūchtā ki 'māṃ, mere abbā, kahāṃ haiṃ?' tab maiṃ uttar detī ki, 'abhāge, terī paidāiś ke pahle hī tere abbā bahiśt kī or cale gae.')

I was unfortunate since birth,[19] there is no doubt about this; if not, I [undoubtedly] would not know so much misery. (Ugra)

मैं ईश्वर के घर से ही अभागिनी बनाकर भेजी गई हूँ; इसमें कोई सन्देह नहीं; अन्यथा मेरी इतनी दुर्दशा न होती। (maiṃ īśvar ke ghar se hī abhāginī banākar bhejī gaī hūṃ; ismeṃ koī sandeh nahīṃ; anyathā merī itnī durdaśā na hotī.)

The perfect participle (वर्तमानकालिक कृदन्त vartamānkālik kṛdant) is used independently to indicate that an action happened one time in the past (see VI.3.2.).

VI.5. THE DOUBLE USAGE OF होना (HONĀ)

To express a general truth, one can use the verb होना (honā) twice, by combining the present participle of होना (honā) with a conjugated form of होना (honā).

Example:

There are seven days in a week.

एक हफ़्ते में सात दिन होते हैं। (ek hafte meṃ sāt din hote haiṃ.)

It is important to note that this construction is also used for things that are not accepted as general truths, but when the speaker in a discussion wants to make his argument more convincing.

Examples:

An ascetic obtains satisfaction through the success of his ascetic fervor. (Ugra)

तपस्वी को अपनी तपस्या की सफलता से आत्म-सन्तोष की प्राप्ति होती है। (tapasvī ko apnī tapasyā kī saphaltā se ātma-santoṣ kī prāpti hotī hai.)

19. Lit.: I was sent unfortunate from God's house.

Sir, our family tree begins directly in Arabia. (*a man claiming to be related to Prophet Muhammad, while this is doubtful to be true*) (Bismillāh)

साहब हमारा शजरा सीधे अरब से शुरू होता है। (sāhab hamārā śajarā sīdhe arab se śurū hotā hai.)

VI.6. SOME IRREGULAR AND ALTERNATIVE VERBAL FORMS

VI.6.1. THE VERB होना (HONĀ) 'TO BE'

Table 29. Conjugation of होना (honā) 'to be': Irregular forms

	PRESENT	IMPFCT. PAST	SUBJUNCTIVE	FUTURE[1]	PFCT. PART.
1 sg.	हूँ (hūṃ)	था/थी (thā/thī)	होऊँ (hoūṃ)	होऊँगा/हूँगा (h(o)ūṃgā/ī)	हुआ/हई (huā/huī)
2 sg.	है (hai)	था/थी (thā/thī)	हो(वे) (ho(ve))	होवेगा/होगा (ho(ve)gā/ī)	हुआ/हुई (huā/huī)
3 sg.	है (hai)	था/थी (thā/thī)	हो(वे) (ho(ve))	होवेगा/होगा (ho(ve)gā/ī)	हुआ/हुई (huā/huī)
1 pl.	हैं (haiṃ)	थे/थीं (the/thīṃ)	हो(वे)ं (ho(ve)ṃ)	होवेंगे/होंगे (ho(ve)ṃge/ī)	हुए/हुईं (hue/huīṃ)
2 pl.	हो (ho)	थे/थीं (the/thīṃ)	हो (ho)[2]	होगे/होओगे (ho(o)ge/ī)	हुए/हुईं (hue/huīṃ)
3 pl.	हैं (haiṃ)	थे/थीं (the/thīṃ)	हो(वे)ं (ho(ve)ṃ)	होवेंगे/होंगे (ho(ve)ṃge/ī)	हुए/हुईं (hue/huīṃ)

[1] Only m. forms are given here. For f. forms, see Tables 27–28.

[2] Exceptionally, one can come across the form होओ (ho-o).

VI.6.2. SOME IMPORTANT IRREGULAR VERBAL FORMS

In the table on the next page, only the irregular forms of a few important verbs are included.

Table 30. Some important irregular verbal forms

	PFCT. PART.	SUBJUNCTIVE/FUTURE[1]	IMPERATIVE
'to do' करना (karnā)	किया/की/किए[2]/कीं kiyā/kī/ki(y)e/kīṃ		कीजिए(गा) kījie(gā)
'to go' जाना (jānā)	गया/गई/गये/गईं gayā/gaī/ga(y)e/gaīṃ	alongside the regular forms, the following irregular forms also occur: जाय (jāy) for जाए (jāe) जायँ (jāyaṃ) for जाएँ (jāeṃ) जायगा (jāygā) for जाएगा (jāegā)	
'to give' देना (denā)	दिया/दी/दिए/दीं diyā/dī/di(y)e/dīṃ	दूँ(गा)/दे(गा)/दें(गे)/दो(गे) dūṃ(gā)/de(gā)/deṃ(ge)/do(ge)	दो/दीजिए(गा) do/dījie(gā)
'to drink' पीना (pīnā)	पिया/पी/पिए/पीं piyā/pī/pi(y)e/pīṃ		पिओ/पीजिए(गा) pio/pījie(gā)
'to take' लेना (lenā)	लिया/ली/लिए/लीं liyā/lī/li(y)e/līṃ	लूँ(गा)/ले(गा)/लें(गे)/लो(गे) lūṃ(gā)/le(gā)/leṃ(ge)/lo(ge)	लो/लीजिए(गा) lo/lījie(gā)

[1] The subjunctive 3 sg. of verbs with a stem ending in -आ (ā), sometimes take the glide -v- between the stem and the ending when the ending starts with a vowel, e.g., आवे (āve) for आए (āe).

[2] When the stem ends in -आ (ā), -ओ (o), -ए (e), or -ई (ī) and the ending starts with -ए (e), a glide -y- can be inserted, e.g., गए or गये, सोए or सोये. This sometimes also occurs with roots ending in -ई (ī), -ई< (īṃ), -ओ (o), एं (eṃ), e.g., आए (āe)/आये (āye); आई/(āī) आयी (āyī); आएगा (āegā)/आयेगा (āyegā).

Note: If the stem ends in -ऊ (-ū) or -ई (-ī), these vowels shorten before endings starting with a vowel.

VI.7. CAUSATIVE AND DOUBLE CAUSATIVE VERBS (प्रेरणार्थ क्रिताएँ PRERAṆĀRTH KRITĀEṂ)

A causative verb is used when one wants to express that an action or state was caused by somebody or something either by an intermediary or through an instrument. When translating to English, often the verbs 'cause to', 'let', 'make', 'have', 'get', or 'help' can be added to the basic meaning of the verb, e.g., 'to cut' vs. 'to cause to cut'; 'to be cut' vs. 'to cause to be cut' (i.e., to actively cut).

Many verbs form semantic pairs in which an intransitive and transitive verb are connected in meaning, but one takes a direct object and the other does not, e.g., “the candle is lit” (i.e., burning) vs. “she lights the candle” (i.e., she makes the candle burn). Other verb pairs are both transitive, but one only takes one object, while the counterpart of the pair takes two objects, e.g., ‘she studies Hindi’ vs. ‘she makes them study Hindi’. In the latter case, the verb often expresses the fact that somebody causes a second or even third party to do something: “she will make the servant prepare the food” vs. “she will make her daughter make the servant prepare the food.” Such verbs are called double causative verbs. Most verbs can be made into a causative and/ or double causative verb in Hindi.

The accurate use of the (double) causative verb can be slightly confusing at first for the English-speaking learner of Hindi, because English often uses ambitransitive verbs. This means that English has verbs that are both transitive and intransitive, without a morphological distinction between them, e.g., the verb ‘to stop’ can be used intransitively (e.g., “the rain stopped” = came to a stop), as well as transitively (e.g., “he stopped the car” = he made it stop). In Hindi, these verbs form a semantic pair, but they will not be morphologically identical. The two words for the intransitive and transitive ‘to stop’ cannot be used interchangeably. As a consequence, it is important to understand the difference between the members of semantic pairs, triads, or even tetrads. Those semantically connected verbs are formed following certain patterns, which will be discussed below.

VI.7.1. FORMATION

Most verbs of which the stem is monosyllabic and the vowel of the stem ending in a consonant is short or of which the stem is dissyllabic are made causative by adding -आ- (-ā-) following the stem:

करना (karnā) ‘to do’ > कराना (karānā) ‘to cause to do’
लिखना (likhnā) ‘to write’ > लिखाना (likhānā) ‘to cause to write’
बदलना (badalnā) ‘to change’ > बदलाना (badlānā) ‘to cause to change’

A double causative is formed by adding -वा- (-vā-) following the stem of intransitive verbs or the stem of transitive verbs with one object of which no intransitive form exists.

Examples:

करना (karnā) 'to do' > करवाना (karvānā) 'to make a second party cause a third party to do'

लिखना (likhnā) 'to write' > लिखवाना (likhvānā) 'to make a second party cause a third party to write'

बदलना (badalnā) 'to change' > बदलवाना (badalvānā) 'to make a second party cause a third party to change'

However, there are a rather large number of exceptions to this general rule. When it comes to stems that have a short vowel, several patterns can be discerned.

Table 31. Causative of stems with a short vowel

		CAUSATIVE	DOUBLE CAUSATIVE
Lengthening	कटना (kaṭnā) to be cut	काटना (kāṭnā) to cut	कटवाना (kaṭvānā) to cause to cut
Guṇa[1]	खुलना (khulnā) to be open	खोलना (kholnā) to open	खुलवाना (khulvānā) to have it opened
Vṛddhi[2]	खिंचना (khiṃcnā) to be drawn	खैंचना[3] (khaiṃcnā) to pull	खिंचवाना (khiṃcvānā) to cause to be pulled
ट > ड़ (ṭ>ṛ)	फटना (phaṭnā) to be torn	फाड़ना (phāṛnā) to tear	फड़वाना (phaṛvānā) to cause to tear

[1] Guṇa or 'quality' is a term from Sanskrit grammar to indicate a change in vowel length. It means that the following vowel shifts can occur: -i- or -ī- > -e-; -u- or -ū- > -o-; and -ṛ- > -ar-.

[2] Vṛddhi or 'increase, enhancement' is the Sanskrit term that is used to indicate lengthening of a vowel that actually builds on the *guṇa* form: -a- > -ā-; -i- or -ī- > -ai-; -u- or -ū- > -au-; -ṛ- > -ār-. Scharpé, *Sanskrit*, 3.

[3] There is also a parallel form खींचना (khīṃcnā).

Stems with a long vowel can also be subject to consonant changes.

Table 32. Causative of stems with a long vowel

		CAUSATIVE	DOUBLE CAUSATIVE
ट > ड़ (ṭ > ṛ)	टूटना (ṭūṭnā) to be broken	तोड़ना (toṛnā) to break	तुड़ाना (tuṛānā) to cause to break
	छूटना (chūṭnā) to be free	छोड़ना (choṛnā) to free, let go	छुड़ाना (chuṛānā) to get released
	फूटना (phūṭnā) to break, burst	फोड़ना (phoṛnā) to cause to break, burst	फुड़वाना (phuṛvānā) to make X break Y

Stems with a long vowel can also change following certain patterns.

Table 33. Causative of stems with a long vowel: Alternatives

		CAUSATIVE	DOUBLE CAUSATIVE
Shortening	जागना (jāgnā) to awake	जगाना (jagānā) to wake someone up	जगवाना (jagvānā) to cause to wake up
	बोलना (bolnā) to speak	बुलाना (bulānā) to call (to summon)	बुलवाना (bulvānā) to send for, cause to be called
Insertion of -ला-(lā-) and -लवा- (-lvā-), mostly with stems ending in a vowel	पीना (pīnā) to drink	पिलाना (pilānā) to make drink	पिलवाना (pilvānā) to make X make Y drink
	खाना (khānā) to eat	खिलाना (khilānā) to feed (make X eat)	खिलवाना (khilvānā) to make X feed
	देना (denā) to give	दिलाना (dilānā) to cause to give	दिलवाना (dilvānā) to make X make Y give
	सोना (sonā) to sleep	सुलाना (sulānā) to cause to sleep	सुलवाना (sulvānā) to cause to sleep
Insertion of -ला-(lā-) and -लवा- (-lvā-), also with stems ending in a consonant	कहना (kahnā) to speak	कहाना (kahāna) / कहलाना (kahlānā) to cause to say	कहलवाना (kahalvānā) to cause to say

(continued)

Table 33. Causative of stems with a long vowel: Alternatives *(continued)*

		CAUSATIVE	DOUBLE CAUSATIVE
Combination of the above rules	सीखना (sīkhnā) to study	सिखाना (sikhāna)/ सिखलाना (sikhlānā) to teach	सिखवाना (sikhvānā) to make X teach
	देखना (dekhnā) to see	दिखाना (dikhānā)/ दिखलाना (dikhlānā) to show	दिखवाना (dikhvānā) to make X show
	रोना (ronā) to cry	रुलाना (rulānā) to make X cry	रुलवाना (rulvānā) to make X make Y cry
	बैठना (baiṭhnā) to sit	बिठाना (biṭhānā)/ बिठलाना (biṭhlānā) to cause to sit, to seat	बिठवाना (biṭhvānā) to make X seat Y
	धुलना (dhulnā) to be washed	धोना (dhonā) to wash	धुलाना (dhulānā)/ धुलवाना (dhulvānā) to make X wash
	खेलना (khelnā) to play	खिलाना (khilānā) to cause to play	खिलवाना (khilvānā) to make X make Y play

A few other combined irregularities are shown in the table below.

Table 34. Causative with combined irregularities

		CAUSATIVE	DOUBLE CAUSATIVE
Shortening + -वा- (vā)	लेना (lenā) to take	लिवाना (livānā) to cause to take	
Shortening + न > त (n > t)	जानना (jānnā) to know	जनाना (janānā)/जताना (jatānā)/जतलाना (jatlānā) to make known, inform	जतलवाना (jatalvānā) to have X informed
Guṇa + क>च (k > c)	बिकना (biknā) to be sold	बेचना (becnā) to sell	बिकाना (bikānā) to cause X to sell

Notes:

1. It is important to know that all causative verbs are transitive (see VI.3.2.).

2. Note that sometimes the meaning of the members of semantic

pairs can over time become (seemingly) unrelated, e.g., सुनना (sunnā) 'to hear' vs. सुनाना (sunānā) 'to narrate'; समझना (samajhnā) 'to understand' vs. समझाना (samjhānā) 'to explain'.

3. Sometimes the meaning of the causative and double causative verbs can largely overlap.

4. With causative verbs, the person who is made or caused to do something will be followed in Hindi by को. With double causative verbs that have two objects, the intermediary will be followed in Hindi by से (se) or के द्वारा (ke dvārā). E.g., माताजी अपनी बेटी से कुत्ते को खाना खिलवाती है। (mātājī apnī beṭī se kutte ko khānā khilvātī hai) 'The mother makes her daughter feed the dog'.

5. It is important to note that some very common verbs, like आना (ānā) 'to come' and जाना (jānā) 'to go' do not have causative or double causative forms. If you want to express that, e.g., you will make somebody come to your house, you would use alternative verbs like बुलाना (bulānā) or पुकारना (pukārnā) 'invite, summon, call', if you make somebody go, you would use the verb भेजना (bhejnā) 'to send'.

Examples:

The house is burning (on fire) (verb expressing a state, not action). The son sets the house on fire (lit.: makes burn). The father makes his son set the house on fire.

घर जलता है। बेटा घर जलाता है। पिता बेटे से घर जलवाता है। (ghar jaltā hai. beṭā ghar jalātā hai. pitā beṭe se ghar jalvātā hai.)

The girl is drinking milk. Her mother always makes the girl drink milk. The mother makes the servant make the girl drink milk.

लड़की दूध पी रही है। माता-जी हमेशा लड़की को दूध पिलाती है। माता-जी नौकरानी से लड़की को दूध पिलवाती है। (laṛkī dūdh pī rahī hai. mātā-jī hameśā laṛkī ko dūdh pilātī hai. mātā-jī naukarānī se laṛkī ko dūdh pilvātī hai.)

While playing, the older brother broke the smaller brother's leg. Now, the younger brother's leg is broken.

खेलते-खेलते बड़े भाई ने छोटे भाई के पैर को तोड़ दिया है। अभी छोटे भाई का पैर टूटा है। (khelte-khelte baṛe bhāī ne choṭe bhāī ke pair ko toṛ diyā hai. abhī choṭe bhāī kā pair ṭūṭā hai.)

The car did not come to a stop before the house, so my sister stopped the car. The police had stopped her car.

गाड़ी घर के सामने नहीं रुकी तो मेरी बहन ने गाड़ी को रोका। पुलिस ने पहले ही उसकी गाड़ी रुकवाई थी। (gāṛī ghar ke sāmne nahīṃ rukī to merī bahan ne gāṛī ko rokā. pulis ne pahle hī uskī gāṛī rukvāī thī.)

VII. LIGHT VERBS, COLORING VERBS, (COMPOUND) AUXILIARY VERBS, VECTOR VERBS (सहायक क्रिया SAHĀYAK KRIYĀ)

Hindi makes use of compound verbs, in which the vector verb loses its own original meaning, but adds some nuance ('color') to the first (main) verb of the compound. The vector verb is the part of the compound verb that shows the tense, gender, and number of the verb. The vector verb will be combined with a stem-absolutive, stem, present participle, past participles, verbal noun, or infinitive, adding a specific dimension to the original meaning of the main verb.[1]

VII.1. आना (ĀNĀ) 'TO COME'

Stem-absolutive	+	आना (ānā)	→	emphasizes the original meaning of the main verb (often a verb of movement)
Pfct. part.	+	आना (ānā)	→	action is in progress
Infinitive	+	आना (ānā)	→	'to know how'

Stem-absolutive + आना (ānā):[2] In this combination, the main verb is often a verb of motion. It emphasizes the meaning of the main verb but puts extra emphasis on the fact that the action has been completed. In some contexts, आना (ānā) can emphasize that the motion embedded in the main verb is directed toward the subject or speaker, e.g., भाग आना (bhāg ānā) 'to come running' toward the subject or speaker. The combination of ले (le) + आना (ānā) means 'to take along', which can be literally translated as 'to come, after/while having taken'; पहुँच आना (pahuṃc ānā) 'to reach', लौट आना (lauṭ ānā) 'to return', निकल आना (nikal ānā) 'to appear, get out off, protrude'.

1. Peter Hook dedicated an entire book to this topic: *The Compound Verb in Hindi*. For more in-depth information and more examples, this work should be consulted.
2. See Hook, *Compound Verb*; Agnihotri, *Essential Hindi*, 206; McGregor, *Outline of Hindi*, 114; Schmidt, *Essential Urdu*, 155; Hautli-Janisz, *Urdu/Hindi Motion Verbs*, 136ff.

Examples:

Some saliva had entered his throat, because of which he started coughing. (Rākeś)

उसके गले में थोड़ा झाग उठ आया जिससे उसे खांसी आ गई। (uske gale meṃ thoṛā jhāg uṭh āyā jisse use khāṃsī ā gaī.)

His lower lip protruded a little. (Rākeś)

उसका निचला होंठ थोड़ा बाहर को फैल आया। (uskā niclā hoṃṭh thoṛā bāhar ko phail āyā.)

He has returned from Africa.

वह ऐफ़्रिका से लौट आया है। (vah aifrikā se lauṭ āyā hai.)

I have brought her/him/it with me.

मैं उसको अपने साथ ले आया हूँ। (maiṃ usko apne sāth le āyā hūṃ.)

Perfect participle + आना (ānā): The verb चला आना (calā ānā) 'to come, move along' is the most prevalently used example.

Example:

Return when your work is done. (*Lit.: upon completing the work*)

काम समाप्त हो जाने पर चली आना। (kām samāpt ho jāne par calī ānā.)

Infinitive + आना (ānā): This combination with the logical subject being followed by को (ko) expresses skill or lack thereof. If there is an object expressed with the verb, the object becomes the subject of the sentence:

Examples:

The small children do not know how to swim.

छोटे बच्चों को तैरना नहीं आता है। (choṭe baccoṃ ko tairnā nahīṃ ātā hai.)

I know how to read and write Urdu.

मुझे उर्दू पढ़नी और लिखनी आती है। (mujhe urdū paṛhnī aur likhnī ātī hai.)

Note: आना (ānā) is an intransitive verb; hence, the ने (ne) construction is never used.

VII.2. उठना (UṬHNĀ) 'TO GET UP'

Stem	+	उठना (uṭhnā)	→	emphasizes the unexpected character of the occurrence of the action; intensifies the meaning of the main verb

Stem + उठना (uṭhnā): This emphasizes the unexpected character of the occurrence of the action. The main verb often expresses an emotion (to cry, to startle, to shout), and the combination with उठना (uṭhnā) intensifies its meaning (see also VII.10.).

Examples:

The girl called out: "It's this way!"
लड़की बोल उठी: "इधर है!" (laṛkī bol uṭhī: "idhar hai!")

Ṭinnū started to tremble out of fear for his father. (Bismillāh)
टिन्नू अपने बाप के भय से कांप उठा। (ṭinnū apne bap ke bhay se kāṃp uṭhā.)

Her jealousy (*lit.: the fire of her heart*) flared up.
उसके दिल की आग जल उठी। (uske dil kī āg jal uṭhī.)

The memory of that lover is [suddenly] awoken in my heart. (Varmā)
उस प्रेमी की स्मृति मेरे हृद्य में जाग उठती है। (us premī kī smṛti mere hṛdya meṃ jāg uṭhtī hai.)

Note: उठना (uṭhnā) is an intransitive verb; hence the ने (ne) construction is never used, even if the main verb is transitive.

VII.3. करना (KARNĀ) 'TO DO, MAKE'

Verbal noun	+	करना (karnā)	→	frequent

Verbal noun[3] **+ करना (karnā):** This combination is called the frequent, and it is used to indicate that the action is a habit or something that occurs frequently. Often, it is translated with 'used to' when the vector verb is put in a past form or by the addition of 'frequently' or 'habitually' when it is put in the present. Actions that will be a regularity or pattern in the future can be expressed by combining the perfect participle ending in -आ (-ā) with the future tense of करना (karnā).

As the perfect tense is used to indicate completed, isolated actions, this is contrary to the inherent character of a frequent and hence the main verb will normally not occur in the perfect tense.

Examples:

It was summer. Everybody slept outside. Only the women used to sleep inside. (Bismillāh)

गर्मी के दिन थे। सभी लोग बाहर सोते थे। सिर्फ़ औरतें भीतर सोया करती थीं। (garmī ke din the. sabhī log bāhar sote the. sirf auratem̥ bhītar soyā kartī thīm̥.)

She (*plural is used to show respect*) kept looking back while turning around. (Varmā)

वे बीच बीच में मुड़कर पीछे भी देख लिया करती थीं। (ve bīc bīc mem̥ mur̥kar pīche bhī dekh liyā kartī thīm̥.)

Come and sit under this tree every noon. I will throw down a few fresh apples for you. (Gulzār)

रोज़ दोपहर को इसी पेड़ के नीचे आ जाया कर। मैं कुछ सेब तेरे लिए फेंक दिया करूँगा। (roz dopahar ko isī per̥ ke nīce ā jāyā kar. maim̥ kuch seb tere lie phem̥k diyā karūm̥gā.)

Note: The verb जाना (jānā) has a verbal noun that is not identical to the perfect participle गया (gayā), but has an irregular verbal noun जाया (jāyā).

3. Mostly, a verbal noun looks the same as a perfect participle ending in -आ (-ā). It can be translated as the English verbal form ending in -ing, used as a noun. E.g., "He usually does the talking": 'talking' is a verbal noun.

VII.4. चाहना (CĀHNĀ) 'TO WANT, TO WISH'

Infinitive	+	चाहना (cāhnā)	→	'to wish', 'to want'

Infinitive + चाहना (cāhnā): This combination is used to express a wish. Bear in mind that चाहना (cāhnā) is a transitive verb, so in the perfective tense, the ने (ne) construction will be used, even if the main verb is intransitive.

In the present tense, the infinitive always ends in -ना (-nā). However, when चाहना (cāhnā) is put in a perfective tense and the main verb is a transitive verb, the infinitive will agree in number and gender with the object of the infinitive when the object is not followed by को (ko). When the object is followed by को (ko), or the main verb is intransitive, the infinitive always ends in -ना (nā).

Examples:

I don't want to forget my lovers. (Varmā)
मैं अपने प्रेमियों को नहीं भूलना चाहती। (maiṃ apne premiyoṃ ko nahīṃ bhūlnā cāhtī.)

Pardon me, Mister Siddiqī, I want to know one thing. (Bismillāh)
माफ़ कीजिएगा सिद्दीक़ी साहब, मैं एक बात जानना चाहता हूँ। (māf kījiegā siddīqī sāhab, maiṃ ek bāt jānnā cāhtā hūṃ.)

She wanted to buy that book, but [she had] no money at that time.
उसने उस किताब को ख़रीदना चाहा, लेकिन उस वक़्त पैसे नहीं थे। (usne us kitāb ko kharīdnā cāhā, lekin us vaqt paise nahīṃ the.)

VII.5. चाहिए (CĀHIE) 'IT IS DESIRABLE, WANTED, NEEDED'

Infinitive	+	चाहिए (cāhie)	→	'ought to', 'should', 'need'

Infinitive + चाहिए (cāhie): This combination expresses an obligation or need. Often, the obligation is a moral one (see V.8.1.).[4]

4. This is a historic passive form of the verb चाहना (cāhnā) and never changes when used in this sense.

The constituent of the sentence that is the subject in English is followed by को (ko) in Hindi and hence cannot be the grammatical subject in Hindi. As a result, when there is an object to the main verb, this object will become the grammatical subject, and the infinitive will agree in number and gender with this object when the object is not followed by को (ko).

To express an obligation in the past, the past tense of होना (honā) can be added. If the infinitive agrees with the direct object, the past form of होना (honā) will also agree. When the infinitive does not agree, the past form of होना (honā) will occur in the 3 m. sg.

If the main clause contains चाहिए (cāhie), and it is followed by the conjunct कि (ki), the subordinate clause following the कि (ki) will often be put in the subjunctive case.

Examples:

You should talk [in] Hindi.
आपको हिन्दी बोलनी चाहिए। (āpko hindī bolnī cāhie.)

I should read that book.
मुझे उस किताब को पढ़ना चाहिए। (mujhe us kitāb ko paṛhnā cāhie.)

Should Urdu have been the national language?
क्या उर्दू राष्ट्राभाषा होनी चाहिए थी? (kyā urdū rāṣṭrābhāṣā honī cāhie thī?)

He should learn Hindi.
उसको चाहिए कि वह हिन्दी सीख ले। (usko cāhie ki vah hindī sīkh le.)

Sometimes, one comes across the word चाहिए (cāhie) translated as 'want', e.g., आप को क्या चाहिए? (āp ko kyā cāhie?), translated as "What do you want?" Strictly speaking, this is inaccurate, and the more precise translation would be "What do yo need?" Of course, wants and needs can overlap, and hence one could state that there are instances in which they could be used interchangeably. However, it is more accurate to use the conjugated form of चाहना (cāhnā) to express wants, and चाहिए (cāhie) to express needs.

VII.6. चुकना (CUKNĀ) 'TO BE FINISHED, COMPLETED'

Stem	+	चुकना (cuknā)	→	indicates that the action is completed

Stem + चुकना (cuknā): The combination of a stem of the main verb with the auxiliary verb चुकना indicates that the action has been completed. Often, the word 'already' can be added in the English translation. Most often, the perfect tense will be used. As this construction emphasizes completion, the verb चुकना (cuknā) is generally not found in the continuous or imperfect tense.

Note: चुकना (cuknā) is an intransitive verb, so the ने (ne) construction is never used in the perfective tense.

Examples:

His sleep had already been disrupted. (Bismillāh)
नींद उसकी उखड़ चुकी थी। (nīṃd uskī ukhaṛ cukī thī.)

The stuff made of metal and wood had long been removed from it. (Rākeś)
लोहे और लकड़ी का सामान उसमें से कब का निकाला जा चुका था। (lohe aur lakṛī kā sāmān usmeṃ se kab kā nikālā jā cukā thā.)

I (f.) have already eaten.
मैं खाना खा चुकी हूँ। (maiṃ khānā khā cukī hūṃ.)

They may have eaten already.
वे खाना खा चुके होवेंगे। (ve khānā khā cuke hoveṃge.)

He had accepted the death of Cirāg and his wife and kids for some time. (Rākeś)
चिराग और उसके बीवी-बच्चों की मौत को वह काफ़ी पहले स्वीकार कर चुका था। (cirāg aur uske bīvī-baccoṃ kī maut ko vah kāfī pahle svīkār kar cukā thā.)

VII.7. जाना (JĀNĀ) 'TO GO'

Intransitive stem	+	जाना (jānā)	→	change in condition
Transitive stem	+	जाना (jānā)	→	completion
Present participle	+	जाना (jānā)	→	progressive, action with a certain duration
Past participle ending in -ए (-e)	+	जाना (jānā)	→	intensive
Past participle	+	जाना (jānā)	→	passive

Intransitive stem + जाना (jānā): This expresses a change in condition. In combination with an intransitive verb, the meaning of the primary verb is emphasized. In combination with verbs of motion, it stresses the fact that the action is developing. A few common combinations are हो जाना (ho jānā) 'to become', बैठ जाना (baiṭh jānā) 'to sit down', सो जाना (so jānā) 'to go to sleep', मर जाना (mar jānā) 'to die', आ जाना (ā jānā) 'to come', भाग जाना (bhāg jānā) 'to flee'.

Examples:

My sense of judgement had died. (Yaśpāl)
मेरा विवेक मर गया था। (merā vivek mar gayā thā.)

He will come to know the entire event. (Yaśpāl)
उसे सारी घटना का पता चल जाएगा। (use sārī ghaṭnā kā patā cal jāegā.)

When I arrived there, I felt as if I had arrived at the right place. (Yaśpāl)
वहाँ पहुँच कर मुझे अनुभव हुआ मानो एक ठिकाने पहुँच गया हूँ। (vahāṃ pahuṃc kar mujhe anubhav huā māno ek ṭhikāne pahuṃc gayā hūṃ.)

Natthu became worried. (Gulzār)
नथ्थू परेशान हो गया। (natthu pareśān ho gayā.)

A few times, the tongues of both got burned. (Premcand)
कई बार दोनों की ज़बानें जल गईं। (kaī bār donoṃ kī zabāneṃ jal gaīṃ.)

Transitive stem + जाना (jānā): This combination implies that the action has been completed or is carried through. The inherent meaning of the main verb is also emphasized. A few common examples are खा जाना (khā jānā) 'to eat up', पी जाना (pī jānā) 'to drink up', पढ़ जाना (paṛh jānā) 'to read through', भूल जाना (bhūl jānā) 'to forget', छोड़ जाना (choṛ jānā) 'to leave behind'.

Examples:

While tasting, Nathnī devoured all the apples. (Gulzār)
देखते-देखते नथनी सारे सेब चट कर गई। (dehte-dekhte nathnī sāre seb caṭ kar gaī.)

I did not have that key—it was lost. (Yaśpāl)
वह चाबी मेरे पास थी नहीं - खो गयी। (vah cābī mere pās thī nahīṃ—kho gayī.)

[If he] would come into [my] possession, I could swallow him in one gulp! (*a crocodile dreaming about eating a monkey*) (Gulzār)
हाथ लग जाए तो एक ही घूँठ में सुड़क जाऊँ। (hāth lag jāe to ek hī ghūṃṭh meṃ suṛak jāūṃ.)

Present participle + जाना (jānā): This is progressive and expresses that the action is ongoing and has a certain duration. Often, this combination can also imply that the act is carried on with a certain purpose or that the continuation of the act leads to a change in condition.[5]

Examples:

Khilāvan heard from afar the sound of their moving along, but that sound slowly became softer. (Varmā)
दूर से उनके चलने की आवाज़ खिलावन को सुनाई पड़ रही थी, पर वह आवाज़ धीरे-धीरे हल्की होती जाती थी। (dūr se unke calne kī āvāz khilāvan ko sunāī paṛ rahī thī, par vah āvāz dhīre-dhīre halkī hotī jātī thī.)

As the darkness grew, the atmosphere of excitement in the drinking house also increasingly grew. (Premcand)
ज्यों-ज्यों अंधेरा बढ़ता था, मधुशाला की रौनक भी बढ़ती जाती थी। (jyoṃ-jyoṃ andherā baṛhtā thā, madhuśālā kī raunak bhī baṛhtī jātī thī.)

5. Schmidt, *Essential Urdu*, 123; McGregor, *Outline of Hindi*, 150.

I kept on working and he kept on watching.
मैं काम करती गई और वह देखता गया। (maiṃ kām kartī gaī aur vah dekhtā gayā.)

The child kept on playing.
बच्चा खेलता गया। (baccā kheltā gayā.)

Past participle in -ए (-e) + जाना (jānā):

1. The perfect participle ending invariably in -ए (-e) combined with जाना (jānā) also emphasizes that the action is still ongoing and, moreover, has an intensifying effect.

Example:

He keeps saying that he is innocent.
वह कहे जाता है कि मैं निर्दोष हूँ। (vah kahe jātā hai ki maiṃ nirdoṣ hūṃ.)

2. Often, a past participle is combined with a conjugated form of जाना (jānā), both agreeing in gender and number with the subject. This combination is called the passive. Most actions can be expressed in an active and a passive way, e.g., the active construction "The children ate all the sweets" can be rendered into a passive costruction: "All the sweets were eaten by the children."

If the agent is expressed, it is followed by से (se) (sometimes के द्वारा (ke dvārā)). Often, however, the doer of the action will not be expressed ("the car was stolen [by a thief]"). Note that the direct object of the active sentence becomes the subject of the passive sentence.

Examples:

The girl is daily beaten by her brother.
लड़की अपने भाई से रोज़ पीती जाती है। (laṛkī apne bhāī se roz pītī jātī hai.)

A telegram was sent home and everything was fixed. (Yaśpāl)
घर तार दिया गया और सब काम हो गया। (ghar tār diyā gayā aur sab kām ho gayā.)

It is said that...
कहा जाता है कि...(kahā jātā hai ki...)

The stuff made of metal and wood had long been removed from it. (Rākeś)
लोहे और लकड़ी का सामान उसमें से कब का निकाला जा चुका था। (lohe aur lakṛī kā sāmān usmeṃ se kab kā nikālā jā cukā thā.)

Intransitive verbs, which do not have a direct object, are generally put in the passive to show incapability or inability, and are hence most often constructed in the negative. The verb is expressed in the 3 m. sg., as there is no grammatical subject in the sentence. The one who is incapable of conducting the action is constructed with से (se).

Example:

He was unable to sleep. (Lit.: 'sleeping was not done by him')
उससे सोया नहीं गया। (usse soyā nahīṃ gayā.)

Notes:

1. जाना (jānā) is an intransitive verb, and even when combined with a transitive main verb, the ने (ne) construction is never used.

2. When जाना (jānā) is combined as a main verb with the vector verb जाना (jānā) in a passive construction to express the incapability to go, the perfect participle is replaced by the irregular verbal noun जाया (jāyā), e.g., मुझसे जाया नहीं जाएगा (mujh se jāyā nahīṃ jaegā): I will not be able to go.

3. For English speakers, there often is confusion between intransitive verbs (implying a change in condition) and what could be constructed as a passive. Verbs like 'to be cut', 'to be saved', 'to be lost', 'to be placed/kept', etc., can generally be translated with an intransitive verb rather than a passive construction. The passive construction would put heavy emphasis on the action expressed in the verb. Often, such emphasis is unnecessary or even unwarranted.

Example: A mother is preparing a snack for her child. She cuts up an apple and announces that the apple has been cut. Her message would be "the apple is cut up," hence ready to be eaten. In this case, the mother is most likely to announce सेब काटा है (seb kāṭā hai), in which the emphasis is on the fact that the apple is cut up, basically describing its condition. An alternative construction would be सेब कट गया (seb kaṭ gayā), with emphasis on the fact that the apple was first whole, and now is cut into pieces. The passive construction सेब काटा गया (seb kāṭā gayā) would put special emphasis on the fact that the apple was cut by somebody, almost as if one might be looking for the person who conducted the act of cutting, answering the question "By whom was this apple cut up?": सेब किस से काटा गया? (seb kis se kāṭā gayā?). Here, as in many a context, this emphasis would be extremely strong, and one of the former constructions would be preferable in order to accurately express the intended emphasis.

VII.8. डालना (ḌĀLNĀ) 'TO PLACE, THROW, PUT'

Stem	+	डालना (ḍālnā)	→	emphasis, determination, force

Stem + डालना (ḍālnā): This implies that the action occurs either with determination, force, or even violence, or with a certain casualness or indifference.

Examples:

My mirror was trashed [by my in-laws], because I was a widow. (Yaśpāl)
मेरा आईना तोड़ डाला गया क्योंकि मैं विधवा थी। (merā āīnā toṛ ḍālā gayā kyoṃki maiṃ vidhvā thī.)

He killed his enemy.
उसने अपने दुश्मन को मार डाला। (usne apne duśman ko mār ḍālā.)

He destroyed his new bike.
उसने अपनी नई बाइक तोड़ डाली। (usne apnī naī bāik toṛ ḍālī.)

Meanwhile I have [thoughtlessly] done something stupid; will you forgive me? (Varmā)
इस बीच में मैंने एक अनुचित काम कर डाला, मुझे क्षमा करोगी? (is bīc meṃ maiṃne ek anucit kām kar ḍālā, mujhe kṣamā karogī?)

Note: डालना (ḍālnā) is a transitive verb. When the combination is used in the perfect tense, the ने (ne) construction will be used.

VII.9. देना (DENĀ) 'TO GIVE'

Transitive stem	+	देना (denā)	→	action affects somebody else other than the doer
Intransitive stem	+	देना (denā)	→	inchoative (sudden onset)
Pfct. part. ending in -ए (-e)	+	देना (denā)	→	emphasizes the meaning of the main verb
Infinitive ending in -ने (–ne)	+	देना (denā)	→	permission

Transitive stem + देना (denā): This combination of verbs expresses the fact that the action benefits somebody else than the person who is conducting the action or than the subject of the sentence (as opposed to the combination with the verb लेना (lenā)). While it can be hard to render the exact equivalent of this vector verb into English, it is a very important compound verb that can give additional information about the intention of the doer of the action. In the perfective tense, the ने (ne) construction will be used. For additional information through contrast with लेना (lenā), see also VII.15.

Examples:

Give it to me!
मुझ को दे दो! (mujh ko de do!)

Naththu narrated the entire story.[6] (Gulzār)
नथ्थु ने सारी राम कहानी कह दी। (naththu ne sārī rām kahānī kah dī.)

And she did not have her servant throw you out of her room? (Varmā)
और उसने तुम्हें नौकर द्वारा अपने कमरे से निकलवा नहीं दिया? (aur usne tumheṃ naukar dvārā apne kamre se nikalvā nahīṃ diyā?)

---

6. Lit.: 'the entire Rām story': this is a reference to the *Rāmāyana*, implying that it is a long and complicated story.

I will throw down a few fresh apples for you. (Gulzār)

मैं कुछ ताज़ा सेब तेरे लिए फेंक दिया करूँगा। (maiṃ kuch tāzā seb tere lie pheṃk diyā karūṃgā.)

Intransitive stem + देना (denā): In combination with intransitive verbs, the vector verb देना (denā) adds an inchoative aspect, i.e., it emphasizes the very sudden character of the action. In combination with these intransitive verbs, the ने (ne) construction is not used in the perfective tense.

Examples:

The girl burst into tears.

लड़की रो दी। (laṛkī ro dī.)

The boys burst into laughter.

लड़के हँस दिए। (laṛke haṃs diye.)

Perfect participle in -ए (-e) + देना (denā): This verbal sequence intensifies the meaning of the main verb, placing an emphatic tone on the message. This usage is rare, with the exception of the common combination कहे देना (kahe denā).

Examples:

I ensure/warn you. (I am telling you emphatically)

मैं तुम से कहे देता हूँ। (maiṃ tum se kahe detā hūṃ.)

Somebody used to place a kulhaṛ (clay cup) to the mouth of his friend [making him join in the drinking]. (Premcand)

कोई अपने दोस्त के मुँह में कुल्हड़ लगाया देता था। (koī apne dost ke muṃh meṃ kulhaṛ lagāye detā thā.)

Infinitive ending in -ने (-ne) + देना (denā): This combination forms the permissive voice and can be translated in English by 'to allow to', 'to let'. When put in the perfective tense, the ने (ne) construction will in this case always be used, even if the main verb is intransitive.

Examples:

He is ready to consider [our words], but his mother does not allow [him] to consider. (Ugra)

मानने के लिए तो वह तैयार है पर उसकी माँ मानने नहीं देती। (mānne ke liye to vah taiyār hai, par uskī māṃ mānne nahīṃ detī.)

He let the thief go.

उसने चोर को जाने दिया। (usne cor ko jāne diyā.)

Let the secret remain exactly the way it is. (Varmā)

यह रहस्य जैसा है वैसा ही रहने दो। (yah rahasy jaisā hai vaisā hī rahne do.)

VII.10. पड़ना (PAṚNĀ) 'TO FALL', 'TO HAVE TO'

Stem	+	पड़ना (paṛnā)	→	suddenness, unexpected character
Infinitive	+	पड़ना (paṛnā)	→	'to have to'

Stem + पड़ना (paṛnā): This vector verb emphasizes the unexpected character of the occurrence of the action. The main verb often expresses an emotion (to cry, to startle, to shout), and always combines with verbs that can occur suddenly. The combination with पड़ना (paṛnā) should be considered alongside the vector verb उठना (uṭhnā) (see VII.2.).

Examples:

I fell down, having become unconscious. (Ugra)

मैं मूर्छित होकर गिर पड़ी। (maiṃ mūrchit hokar gir paṛī.)

Saying this, she burst out, roaring with laughter, like witches [do]. (Gulzār)

यह कहते हुए वह क़हक़हा मारके हँस पड़ी, डाइनों की तरह। (yah kahte hue vah qahqahā mārke haṃs paṛī, ḍāinoṃ kī tarah.)

Infinitive + पड़ना (paṛnā): This construction is used to express an obligation or compulsion (see V.8.2.). The constituent of the sentence that would be the subject in English is followed by को (ko) in Hindi and, hence, cannot be the grammatical subject in Hindi. As a result, when there is an object to the main verb (i.e., the main verb is a transitive infinitive), this object will become the grammatical subject and the infinitive will agree in number and gender with this object when the object is not followed by को (ko). The vector verb पड़ना (paṛnā) can be conjugated in different tenses.

Examples:

Children have to go to the dentist once a year.
बच्चों को साल में एक बार दन्तचिकित्सक के पास जाना पड़ता है। (baccoṃ ko sāl meṃ ek bār dantcikitsak ke pās jānā paṛtā hai.)

The thief will have to return all the things.
चोर को सब चीज़ें वापस देनी पड़ेंगी। (cor ko sab cīzeṃ vāpas denī paṛeṃgī.)

You had to read those books.
तुम्हें वे किताबें पढ़नी पड़ती थीं। (tumheṃ ve kitābeṃ paṛhnī paṛtī thīṃ.)

Note: पड़ना (paṛnā) is an intransitive verb. As a result, the ने (ne) construction will never be used. (See VII.5. and VII.18. for other ways to express obligations, as well as V.8.2.)

VII.11. पाना (PĀNĀ) 'TO OBTAIN, TO MANAGE'

Stem	+	पाना (pānā)	→	can(not): ability / inability
Infinitive on -ने (ne)	+	पाना (pānā)	→	can(not): ability / inability

Stem + पाना (pānā): This vector verb is used to translate 'can', but in most instances, the emphasis is on (not) being able to complete an action, notwithstanding trying to do so. This is slightly different from the use of the verb सकना (saknā) (see VII.17.), where the emphasis is on the (in)ability to perform the action. Note that sentences with पाना (pānā) are almost always put in the negative.

Examples:

[If I] had not gone to the police station, I may never have been able to make it home. (Yaśpāl)

थाने न जाता तो शायद् कभी घर न पहुँच पाता। (thāne na jātā to śāyad kabhī ghar na pahuṃc pātā.)

Even after a full day, I could not meet with the editor.

एक दिन के बाद् भी मैं संपादक से मिल नहीं पाई। (ek din ke bād bhī maiṃ sampādak se mil nahīṃ pāī.)

The lion could not catch the deer.

शेर हिरन को पकड़ नहीं पाया। (śer hiran ko pakaṛ nahīṃ pāyā.)

You will not be able to buy a ticket for the Christmas break.

तुम क्रिस्मस ब्रेक के लिए् टिकट ख़रीद् नहीं पाओगे। (tum Christmas break ke lie ṭikaṭ kharīd nahīṃ pāoge.)

Infinitive on -ने (-ne) + पाना (pānā): This has the same meaning as the previous construction and is also almost solely used in a negative construction.

Note: Notwithstanding the fact that पाना (pānā) is a transitive verb and would use ने (ne) when functioning as a main verb in the perfective tense, the ने (ne) construction is not used when पाना (pānā) acts as a vector verb in the perfective tense.

VII.12. बैठना (BAIṬHNĀ) 'TO SIT'

Stem	+	बैठना (baiṭhnā)	→	pejorative connotation
Pfct. part. –ए (-e)	+	बैठना (baiṭhnā)	→	pejorative connotation

Stem + बैठना (baiṭhnā): This indicates that an action has happened carelessly, negligently, or even in a dishonest manner.[7] Often, a certain disappointment or deterioration of the situation is suggested. The action is generally regrettable or even condemnable.[8] The use of

7. Sandahl, *Hindi Reference*, 126.
8. McGregor, *Outline of Hindi*, 113.

this vector verb can indicate that the speaker does not approve of the action.[9]

Examples:

The man gambled his wife away. (Lit.: the man lost his wife in a gambling game.)
आदमी जूए की बाज़ी में अपनी बीवी खो बैठा। (ādmī jūe kī bazī meṃ apnī bīvī kho baiṭhā.)

He threw him into the alley and climbed on his chest. (Rākeś)
गली में गिराकर उसकी छाती पर चढ़ बैठा। (galī meṃ girākar uskī chātī par caṛh baiṭhā.)

The army (f.) is fighting old people.
फौज (f.) बूढ़े लोगों से लड़ बैठी है। (fauj būṛhe logoṃ se laṛ baiṭhī hai.)

Perfect participle ending in -ए (-e) + बैठना (baiṭhnā): This combination has the same meaning as the combination with the stem.

Note: बैठना (baiṭhnā) is an intransitive verb, hence the ने (ne) construction will never be used.

VII.13. रखना (RAKHNĀ) 'TO PLACE, TO KEEP'

Stem	+	रखना (rakhnā)	→	action with a lasting result

Stem + रखना (rakhnā): This combination implies that the result of the action is durable, leading to an achievement with a certain duration, either temporary or lasting.

Examples:

Has a cobbler gained possession of that shop now? (Rākeś)
अब इस दुकान को एक मोची ने कब्ज़ा कर रखा है? (ab is dukān ko ek mocī kabzā kar rakhā hai?)

9. Schmidt, *Essential Urdu*, 148.

My father has stopped smoking five weeks ago.

मेरे पिता जी ने पाँच हफ़्ते से सिग्रेट पीना छोड़ रखा है। (mere pitā jī ne pāṃc hafte se sigreṭ pīnā choṛ rakhā hai.)

I have put the plant on the table.

मैं ने पौधा मेज़ पर रख रखा है। (maiṃ ne paudhā mez par rakh rakhā hai.)

Both of them had strangely perplexed me. (*The subject just saw two things that confused him profoundly.*) (Varmā)

इन दोनों ने मुझे एक अजीब चक्कर में डाल रखा था। (in donoṃ ne mujhe ek ajīb cakkar meṃ ḍāl rakhā thā.)

Note: रखना (rakhnā) is a transitive verb. When the combination is used in the perfect tense, the ने (ne) construction will be used.

VII.14. रहना (RAHNĀ) 'TO STAY'

Stem	+	रहना (rahnā)	→	progressive
Prs. part.	+	रहना (rahnā)	→	actions with certain duration (non-stative)
Pfct. part.	+	रहना (rahnā)	→	actions with certain duration (stative)

Stem + रहना (rahnā): This combination forms the continuous tense (see VI.3.3.).

Present participle + रहना (rahnā): The vector verb indicates that the action of the main verb has a certain duration.

Examples:

Kallū was lying down, having covered his face with the sheet, and he kept thinking [for some time]. (Bismillāh)

कल्लू चादर से अपना मुँह ढँके पड़ा रहा और सोचता रहा। (kallū cādar se apnā muṃh ḍhaṃke paṛā rahā aur soctā rahā.)

In between the sound of the belā and sāraṃgī, one can hear the laughter. (Yaśpāl)

बेला और सारंगी की सुर-लहरी के बीच हँसी का कोलहल सुनाई पड़ता रहता है। (belā aur sāraṃgī kī sur-lahrī ke bīc haṃsī kā kolahal sunāī paṛtā rahtā hai.)

Keep on trying!

कोशिश करता रहो! (kośiś kartā raho!)

For two days, Cirāg's house had been scrutinized. (Rākeś)

दो दिन चिराग के घर की छानबीन होती रही थी। (do din cirāg ke ghar kī chānbīn hotī rahī thī.)

The crowd kept looking at him with longing glances. (Bismillāh)

भीड़ उसे हसरत भरी निगाहों से देखती रही। (bhīṛ use hasrat bharī nigāhoṃ se dekhtī rahī.)

Perfect participle + रहना (rahnā) ('to stay'): This is often used in the same way as in combination with the present participle, but this construction is used with verbs that express conditions or states, not actions.

Examples:

Garlands of flowers hang from the upper chambers. (Yaśpāl)

अट्टालिकाओं पर फूलों के गजरे लटके रहते हैं। (aṭṭālikāoṃ par phūloṃ ke gajre laṭke rahte haiṃ.)

The market is filled with the scent of khas and henna. (Yaśpāl)

बाज़ार खस और हिना की गंध से भरा रहता है। (bāzār khas aur hinā kī gandh se bharā rahtā hai.)

Opposite the alley where there used to be a very high beam, there was now a three-story-high building. (Rākeś)

गली के सामने जहां पहले ऊंचे-ऊंचे शहतीर रखे रहते थे, वहां अब एक तिमंजिला मकान खड़ा था। (galī ke sāmne jahāṃ pahle ūṃce-ūṃce śahtīr rakhe rahte the, vahāṃ ab ek timanzilā makān khaṛā thā.)

The lizard keeps sitting on the lookout. (Yaśpāl)

छिपकली ताक लगाये बैठी रहती है। (chipkalī tāk lagāye baiṭhī rahtī hai.)

Note: रहना (rahnā) is an intransitive verb; hence the ने (ne) construction will never be used.

VII.15. लगना (LAGNĀ) 'TO BE ATTACHED TO'

Infinitive ending in –ने (-ne)	+	लगना (lagnā)	→	'to start'

Infinitive ending in -ने (-ne) + लगना (lagnā): This is mostly translated as 'to begin, to start'. Often, लगना (lagnā) is used to indicate the start of an action that does not have an agent, or gives no indication about whether or not the action was started intentionally or with purpose, contrary to transitive verbs like शुरू करना (śurū karnā) 'to start'.

Examples:

Quietly, he started to drink the tea. (Bismillāh)

वह चुपचाप चाय पीने लगा। (vah cupcāp cāy pīne lagā.)

His tongue had become even drier than before, and now his knees started to tremble violently as well. (Rākeś)

ज़बान पहले से और खुश्क हो गई और घुटने भी ज़्यादा काँपने लगे। (zabān pahle se aur khuśk ho gaī aur ghuṭne bhī zyādā kāṃpne lage.)

I started to climb the stairs. (Yaśpāl)

मैं ज़ीने पर चढ़ने लगा। (maiṃ zīne par caṛhne lagā.)

Notes:

1. लगना (lagnā) is intransitive, hence the ने (ne) construction is never used.

2. For the use of लगना (lagnā) in combination with को (ko) to express feelings and emotions, see V.7.1.

VII.16. लेना (LENĀ) 'TO TAKE'

Stem	+	लेना (lenā)	→	action affects the doer

Stem + लेना (lenā): This construction should be considered in constrast to the construction of a stem + देना (denā). The combination of a stem with the vector verb लेना (lenā) expresses the fact that the action benefits or affects the doer of the action, or the subject of the sentence (as opposed to the combination with the verb देना (denā)). While it can be hard to render the exact equivalent of this vector verb into English, it is a very important compound verb that can give additional information about the intention of the doer of the action. In the perfective tense, the ने (ne) construction will be used. For additional information through contrast with देना (denā), see also VII.9.

Examples:

Ṭinnū took the tea. (Bismillāh)
टिन्नू ने चाय ले ली। (ṭinnū ne cāy le lī.)

Every day he used to call out to the people that passed on the street. (Rākeś)
रोज़ वह रास्ते से गुज़रने वाले लोगों को आवाज़ दे-देकर पास बुला लेता था। (roz vah rāste se guzarne vāle logoṃ ko āvāz de-dekar pās bulā letā thā.)

I have written it down. (*so I would not forget, as a reminder to myself*)
मैंने उसको लिख लिया है। (maiṃne usko likh liyā hai.)

When I walk past the kebāb seller, I always have to place a handkerchief over [my] nose. (Yaśpāl)
कबाब फ़रोश के सामने को गुजरते समय नाक पर रूमाल रख लेना पड़ता है। (kabāb faroś ke sāmne ko guzarte samay nāk par rūmāl rakh lenā paṛtā hai.)

Note: लेना (lenā) is a transitive verb. When the verb is put in the perfective tense, the ने (ne) construction will always be used, even if the main verb is intransitive.

VII.17. सकना (SAKNĀ) 'CAN'

Stem	+	सकना (saknā)	→	'can'

Stem + सकना (saknā): This construction is used to express an ability and is generally translated with 'can'. The emphasis in on the ability or inability of the doer of the action to perform the action, or on the possibility for an event to take place. This is slightly different from the use of the verb पाना (pānā) (see VII.11.), where the emphasis is on the (lack of) possibility for the action to be performed, based on circumstances. Stem + सकना (saknā) is also used to ask or give permission to somebody, e.g., 'you can go now'.

Examples:

Can/may I come in?
क्या मैं अन्दर आ सकती हूँ? (kyā maiṃ andar ā saktī hūṃ?)

I don't know why I felt not the least aversion from her, I can't tell. (Yaśpāl)
न जाने क्यों मुझे उसके प्रति ज़रा भी ग्लानि न हुई, कह नहीं सकता। (na jāne kyoṃ mujhe uske prati zarā bhī glāni na huī, kah nahīṃ saktā.)

Now I can no longer meet Cirāg and his wife and children (*i.e., because they are dead*). (Rākeś)
चिराग और उसके बीवी-बच्चे तो अब मुझे मिल नहीं सकते। (cirāg aur bīvī-bacce to ab mujhe mil nahīṃ sakte.)

But until today, I could not find out who was the arsonist. (Rākeś)
मगर आग लगाने वाले का तब से आज तक पता नहीं चल सका था। (magar āg lagāne vāle kā tab se āj tak patā nahīṃ cal sakā thā.)

Note: सकना (saknā) is an intransitive verb. In the perfective tenses, even when used in combination with a transitive main verb, the ने (ne) construction is not used.

VII.18. होना (HONĀ) 'TO BE', 'TO HAVE TO'

Infinitive	+	होना (honā)	→	'to have to'

Infinitive + होना (honā): As explained under the infinitive combined with पड़ना (paṛnā), this construction is used to express an obligation or compulsion. Often, the construction with पड़ना (paṛnā) is considered to be slightly stronger than the one with होना (honā). The construction is identical to that with चाहिए (cāhie). The present or past tense of होना (honā) is added to the infinitive (see V.8.3.).

Examples:

I have to help my sister.
मुझे मेरी बहन की मदद् करनी है। (mujhe merī bahan kī madad karnī hai.)

Will you also have to return home?
क्या आपको भी घर जाना होगा? (kyā āpko bhī ghar jānā hogā?)

I had to work till midnight.
मुझे रात को बारह बजे तक काम करना था। (mujhe rāt ko bārah baje tak kām karnā thā.)

VIII. THE USAGE OF PARTICIPLES (कृदंत KṚDANT)

Participles, often combined with a form of हुआ (huā), can be used:

1. as adjectives ('the **smiling** woman')
2. as nouns ('the **sleeping** [men]')
3. to express a state ('he is **seated**')
4. as an adverb, to express the way in which the action or state expressed by the main verb occurs ('the boy came in [**while**] **laughing**')
5. in time indications

Depending on the way in which participles are used, and whether the participle used is perfective or imperfective, different rules apply when it comes to determining whether the participle will show agreement, or appear in the masculine oblique singular (MOS) form.

Note that in Hindi, the subject of the main verb does not necessarily have to be the same as the subject of the participle. E.g., "The man saw the woman enter the room **while singing**": the singing refers to the D.O., not to the subject.

VIII.1. THE PARTICIPLE USED AS AN ADJECTIVE

Present participles and past participles, often combined with a form of हुआ (huā), can be used as adjectives. The participle used as an adjective will behave like regular adjectives ending in -ā (see III.1. अच्छा (acchā)) and hence only take the endings -ā, -e, and -ī. Grammatically speaking, there is no difference between 'the tall woman' and 'the **smiling** woman'. The participle + हुआ (huā) agree in gender and number with the word it is referring to, whether it precedes or follows the noun.

Imperfect participles are used to describe actions or states that are incomplete or often ongoing ('the **falling** snow'), while perfective participles describe actions that have been completed before the main verb takes place ('the **fallen** snow').

Examples:

Lālū, friend, may I take these remaining apples for my wife? (Gulzar)

लालू, यार, ये बचे हुए सेब मेरी पत्नी के लिये ले जाऊँ? (lālū, yār, ye bace hue seb merī patnī ke liye le jāūṃ?)

She was wearing a printed muslin waistcloth. (Varmā)

छपी हुई मलमल की धोती पहने हुए थी। (chapī huī malmal kī dhotī pahane hue thī.)

The poor prostitutes live upstairs, in dark rooms, hidden behind broken shutters of bamboo. (Yaśpāl)

ऊपर अँधेरी कोठरियों में टूटी हुई चिकों की आड़ में ग़रीब रंडियाँ रहती हैं। (ūpar aṃdherī koṭhariyoṃ meṃ ṭūṭī huī cikoṃ kī āṛ meṃ garīb raṇḍiyāṃ rahtī haiṃ.)

Manorī saw the changed color of his face. (Rākeś)

मनोरी ने उसके चहरे के बदले हुए रंग को देखा। (manorī ne uske cahre ke badle hue rang ko dekhā.)

And Mister Siddīqī got up and started to open the door of the cupboard that had been built into the wall. (Bismillāh)

और सिद्दीक़ी साहब खड़े होकर दीवार में बनी हुई एक अलमारी का दरवाज़ा खोलने लगे। (aur siddīqī sāhab khaṛe hokar dīvār meṃ banī huī ek almārī kā darvāzā kholne lage.)

I was worn out by all that continuous thinking, so I just started to listen to the conversations of the men that were lying nearby. (Yaśpāl)

सोचते-सोचते थक गया तो समीप लेटे हुए आदमियों की बातचीत सुनने लगा। (socte-socte thak gayā to samīp leṭe hue ādmiyoṃ kī bātcīt sunne lagā.)

When he heard this, the listener, sitting inside right next to me, got up. (Rākeś)

उसे सुनकर भीतर बैठा हुआ मेरे साथ वाला श्रोता खड़ा हो गया। (use dekhkar bhītar baiṭhā huā mere sāth vālā śrotā khaṛā ho gayā.)

VIII.2. PARTICIPLES USED AS NOUNS

Participles can also be used as nouns. When a participle is used as a noun, it follows the declension of regular masculine nouns ending in

-ā (see II.1. बेटा (beṭā)). Often, हुआ (huā) will not be expressed explicitly. Note that when हुआ (huā) is implicit, the oblique plural ending -ओं (-oṃ) will be attached to the participle when a plural participle used as a noun is followed by a postposition.

Examples:

How often have I told you a sleeping [person] is not to be woken up, shaking him like this! (Bismillāh)

कितनी बार कहा कि सोते को उस तरह झकझोरकर नहीं जगाया जाता। (kitnī bār kahā ki sote ko is tarah jhakjhorkar nahīṃ jagāyā jātā!)

Take a baked one, don't eat the raw ones!

पक्का ले लो, कच्चों को मत खाओ! (pakkā le lo, kaccoṃ ko mat khāo!)

I won't let that singing [one] (f.) enter.

मैं उस गाती को अन्दर आने नहीं दूँगी। (maiṃ us gātī ko andar āne nahīṃ dūṃgī.)

VIII.3. PARTICIPLES AND THEIR PREDICATIVE USAGE

One instance in which we speak of the predicative usage of the participle is when a participle used as an adjective describes the subject, e.g., "the dog is **lying down**". Often used in sentences where the main verb is होना (honā), the participle is made with verbs that express states and not actions (e.g., to be made, to lie down, to be seated) and hence is also referred to as a stative construction. The हुआ (huā) accompanying the participle may or may not be expressed. The imperfect participle is generally not used for the stative.

Participles of verbs describing a state can also be used predicatively in combination with main verbs other than होना (honā). In this case, the participle will often follow the noun it describes. When used predicatively, the participle generally functions like an adjective, and agrees in gender and number with the noun to which it refers. When the participle follows and qualifies the object rather than the subject, the participle will agree, unless when the object is followed by को (ko), in which case the participle will remain in the masculine singular -ā ending.

Examples:

He is lying down.
वह लेटा हुआ है। (vah leṭā huā hai.)

The door was slightly open. (Bismillāh)
दरवाज़ा थोड़ा खुला हुआ था। (darvāzā thoṛā khulā huā thā.)

When Sir arrived there, he had become very tired. (Bismillāh)
हुज़ूर जब वहाँ पहुँचे तो बहुत थके हुए थे। (huzūr jab vahāṃ pahuṃce to bahut thake hue the.)

The earth, which was covered in darkness, started to shine in the light. (Bismillāh)
धरती, जो अँधेरे में डूबी हुई थी, रौशनी में चमकने लगी। (dhartī, jo andhere meṃ ḍūbī huī thī, rauśnī meṃ camakne lagī.)

I saw that there was dust on every object there. (*Lit.: dust was collected.*) (Bismillāh)
मैंने देखा वहाँ की हर चीज़ पर गर्द जमी हुई थी। (maiṃne dekhā vahāṃ kī har cīz par gard jamī huī thī.)

The people saw that a snake-couple, moving along ardently entangled, came running from the jungle. (Bismillāh)
लोगों ने देखा कि जंगल से साँप का एक जोड़ा, आपस में लिपटा हुआ दौड़ता हुआ आया। (logoṃ ne dekhā ki jaṃgal se sāṃp kā ek joṛā, āpas meṃ lipṭā huā dauṛtā huā āyā.)

One could argue that in the last sentence, 'moving along' describes the action. However, in this sentence, the emphasis is on the fact that the snakes are entangled (perfective, as the action was completed before, now describing a state) and moving (imperfective, ongoing action), not primarily aimed at describing the way in which the action occurs, and hence the participles are used like adjectives rather than adverbs.

VIII.4. THE ADVERBIAL USAGE OF THE PARTICIPLE

Generally, the participle used adverbially provides information about the way the action is conducted, as well as about the subject of the action. E.g., "The woman came in **while singing**." This implies that the action expressed in the participle and the main verb happens simultaneously. Both perfective and imperfect participles can be used adverbially.

The use of an imperfect participle indicates that the action or state is incomplete and/or ongoing at the time the action of the main verb is unfolding (e.g., "He looked around, **while holding** on to the stick [for protection]."). The perfective participle is used for actions or states that were completed before the one expressed by the main verb, and its completion can have an effect that continues at the time the main verb takes place (e.g., "He looked around, [having been] **startled** by the noise.").

At first sight, there seems to be inconsistent information about this aspect of grammar when it comes to whether or not the participle used as an adverb stays invariably in the MOS form (i.e., masculine oblique singular ending in -ए (e)), or agrees in gender and number with the word to which it refers.[1]

Most grammars seem to indicate that the MOS form is used consistently when the participle is used as an adverb. Sandahl[2] indicates that the participle can either agree, appear in the MOS form, or invariably end in -ā, but she does not give any further details, raising the impression that all three options are equal, and that there are no restrictions or special conditions distinguishing their use from one another. Jain also states that the MOS form as well as agreement can occur. If an imperfect participle is used, she suggests that the speaker is only free to choose agreement or the MOS form when the subject is not followed by ने (ne) or को (ko). For perfective participles that do not have their own object and that refer to nouns that are not followed

---

1. Agnihotri, *Essential Hindi*, 234; Jain, *Advanced Hindi*, 7–16; McGregor, *Outline of Hindi*, 175–177; Sandahl, *Hindi Reference*, 107; Schmidt, *Essential Urdu*, 177–178; Snell, *Teach Yourself Hindi*, 232.
2. Sandahl, *Hindi Reference*, 107.

by a postposition, she indicates that the MOS form and the participle showing agreement are interchangeable. Otherwise, Jain,[3] too, states that the MOS form will be used. She concludes the topic of adverbial use of imperfective participles by stating that the MOS form can always be used adverbially, as it will always be correct.

When discussing the topic with native speakers of Hindi, they seem to agree with most published grammars that there is no instance in which using the MOS form for adverbial use is considered 'wrong'. However, there are many instances in which native speakers oppose making the participle used adverbially show agreement.[4]

Alternatively, one could consider that the seeming inconsistencies might have to do more with the interpretation of whether the participle that shows agreement is truly used adverbially. When agreement in gender and number occurs for adverbially used participles, they seem to give more information about the doer of the action than about the way in which the action occurs. While the translation in English might overlap with an adverbial use, in cases where the adverbial participle agrees, one could also interpret that such participles that show agreement are used as an adjective in a predicative way. In other words, rather than emphasizing the simultaneity of two actions or states, or providing a context for the main verb, the participle gives more information about the noun. In a sentence like "Listening to the radio, she cooked dinner", the "listening to the radio" could appear in the MOS form to emphasize the fact that the listening and cooking happen at the same time. However, the participle could occur in

3. Jain, *Advanced Hindi*, 7–16.
4. This conclusion is drawn based upon informal conversations with a small sample of Hindi speakers from the Hindi-speaking belt in Northern India. I do not intend to present this as the result of comprehensive research on the topic. I only want to give an indication of a preliminary impression, based on the way this grammatical topic is presented in published grammars, examples one can find in literary Hindi, and the fact that I noticed over years of teaching and traveling that native speakers seem consistently opposed to cases in which the participle used as an adverb is made to agree in gender and number, while this seems more common and acceptable in written language. This topic needs more extensive and consistent linguistic research before a formal conclusion can be drawn. It is my personal belief that this might be a grammatical feature that is undergoing change, and that the MOS form might be seeing an increase in usage.

feminine singular, agreeing with the subject, if the emphasis is more on the description of the subject, and less so on the circumstances of the main action. In this case, the participle would be used as a predicative adjective, and not adverbially. This interpretation implies that the MOS form and the participle that agrees are not entirely identical, but suggest a slightly different emphasis.

Examples of adverbially used participles in the MOS form:

I saw that she (*the snake*), after she had bitten me and spread her mouth widely, took off satisfied. (Bismillāh)

मैंने देखा वह काटकर अपना फन फैलाए हुए बड़े इतमीनान के साथ चला जा रहा था। (maiṃne dekhā vah kāṭkar apnā phan phailāe hue baṛe itmīnān ke sāth calā jā rahā thā.)

While I washed the feet of this brute with my tears, I said, "Oh dear!" (Ugra)

मैंने, अपने आँसुओं से उस पशु का चरण धोते हुए कहा, 'प्यारे!' (maiṃne, apne āṃsuoṃ se us paśu kā caraṇ dhote hue kahā, 'pyāre!')

While they passed through the narrow bazaars, they were reminding each other of old memories. (Rākeś)

तंग बाज़ारों में से गुज़रते हुए वे एक-दूसरे को पुरानी चीज़ों की याद दिला रहे थे। (taṃg bāzāroṃ meṃ se guzarte hue ve ek-dūsre ko purānī cīzoṃ kī yād dilā rahe the.)

Taking pleasure in his mind of these things, Mādhav spoke: "Now nobody serves such a feast [anymore]." (Premcand)

माधव ने इन पदार्थों का मन-ही-मन मज़ा लेते हुए कहा-अब कोई ऐसा भोज नहीं खिलाता। (mādhav ne in padārthoṃ kā man-hī-man mazā lete hue kahā - ab koī aisā bhoj nahīṃ khilātā.)

Examples of participles showing agreement:

Shakily, I sneaked inside the four walls of the mosque. (Ugra)

मैं काँपती हुई दबे पाँव मस्जिद की चहारदीवारी के भीतर हो गई। (maiṃ kāṃptī huī dabe pāṃv masjid kī cahārdīvārī ke bhītar ho gaī.)

Hunched up and frightened she (*plural for respect*) softly spoke: "Some insect has bitten him." (Bismillāh)

वे दुबकी हुईं, डरी हुईं, मद्धिम आवाज़ में बोलीं: 'उन्हें किसी कीड़े ने काट खाया है।' (ve dubkī huīṃ, ḍarī huīṃ, maddhim āvāz meṃ bolīṃ: 'unheṃ kisī kīṛe ne kāṭ khāyā hai.')

When he saw me crying, the old mullā asked, "Why are you crying, daughter?" (Ugra)

मुझे रोती देखकर वृद्ध मुल्ला ने पूछा: 'क्यों रोती है, बेटी?" (mujhe rotī dekhkar vṛddh mullā ne pūchā: 'kyoṃ rotī hai, beṭī?')

On every street, some group or another of Muslims was seen walking. (Rākeś)

हर सड़क पर मुसलमानों की कोई न कोई टोली घूमती नज़र आ जाती थी। (har saṛak par musalmānoṃ kī koī na koī ṭolī ghūmtī nazar ā jātī thī.)

Two women were scolding each other while screaming. (Rākeś)

दो स्त्रियाँ ऊँची आवाज़ में चीखती हुईं एक-दूसरी को गालियाँ दे रही थीं। (do striyāṃ ūṃcī āvāz meṃ cīkhtī huīṃ ek-dūsrī ko gāliyāṃ de rahī thīṃ.)

A girl of about sixteen years old came running from the alley, grabbed the boy by the arm, and dragged him into the alley. (Rākeś)

एक सोलह-सत्रह साल की लड़की गली के अन्दर से दौड़ती हुई आई और बच्चे को बाँह से पकड़कर गली में ले चली। (ek solah-satrah sāl kī laṛkī galī ke andar se dauṛtī huī āī aur bacce ko bāṃh se pakaṛkar galī meṃ le calī.)

In the following examples, the participles are used in a way that is more descriptive of the doer/subject than of the action.

Examples:

The valuable sarees were kept folded. (Ugra)

कीमती साड़ियाँ तह की हुईं रखी थीं। (qīmatī sāṛiyāṃ tah kī huīṃ rakhī thīṃ.)

'Folded' simply describes the sarees and not the action. The verbs do not really describe actions, but states. Agreement seems to occur more often in such cases.

Some time later, he was seen while entering the room, together with the noble man. (Ugra)

थोड़ी ही देर बाद वह उस सज्जन के साथ उस कमरे में आता दिखाई पड़ा। (thoṛī hī der bād vah us sajjan ke sāth us kamre meṃ ātā dikhāī paṛā.)

'To enter a room' is an action, but the emphasis in this sentence is on the description of the man. The emphasis is not on the act of entering the room while doing something else.

VIII.5. PARTICIPLES USED WHEN INDICATING TIME

1. Present participles ending in -ते (-te) + **ही (hī):** Present participles ending in -ते (-te) (invariably, regardless of the gender or number of the subject or the tense) + the emphatic particle ही (hī) can be translated as 'from the moment, hardly'.

Examples:

I had barely seen the frightening sight of the superintendent of the police with his huge belly, when I came to my senses (*my senses were restored*). (Yaśpāl)

लम्बोदार थानेदार की भीषण मूर्ति देखते ही सुध कुछ ठिकाने आ गयी। (lambodār thānedār kī bhīṣaṇ mūrti dekhte hī sudh kuch ṭhikāne ā gayī.)

The women who were seated on their stools in the alleys picked up their stools and went inside from the moment they heard the news. (Rākeś)

यह ख़बर मिलते ही जो स्त्रियाँ गली में पीढ़े बिछाकर बैठी थीं, वे पीढ़े उठाकर घरों के अन्दर चली गईं। (yah khabar milte hī jo striyāṃ galī meṃ pīṛhe bichākar baiṭhī thīṃ, ve pīṛhe uṭhākar gharoṃ ke andar calī gaīṃ.)

2. Double usage of the participle: The double usage of the participle ending in -ए (-e) has an intensifying effect and indicates the continuity of the action.

Example:

I had grown tired because of the continuous thinking, so I started to listen to the conversation of the people that were lying next to me. (Yaśpāl)

सोचते-सोचते थक गया तो समीप लेटे हुए आदमियों की बातचीत सुनने लगा। (socte-socte thak gayā to samīp leṭe hue ādmiyoṃ kī bātcīt sunne lagā.)

3. Present participle ending in -ए (-e) + समय (samay) / वक़्त (vaqt): This is used to indicate that some actions happen simultaneously or to indicate the moment in which something happens.

Examples:

When you walk by, you bow your head in shame. (*Lit.: 'the moment of walking by'*) (Yaśpāl)

गुज़रते समय शर्म से तुम्हारा सिर झुक जाता है। (guzarte samay tumhārā sir jhuk jātā hai.)

Once upon a time, while hunting (*lit.: 'the moment of the hunt'*), a snake couple appeared before me. (Bismillāh)

एक बार शिकार खेलते वक़्त मेरे सामने साँप का एक जोड़ा आ गया। (ek bār śikār khelte vaqt mere sāmne sāṃp kā ek joṛā ā gayā.)

4. Perfect participle ending in -ए (-e): This is used to indicate that some time has elapsed since the action was completed until now.

Example:

Four full days had elapsed without me eating anything. (*Lit.: 'having placed a crumb of food into the mouth'*)

मुँह में अनाज का दाना डाले पूरे चार रोज़ हो गये थे। (muṃh meṃ anāj kā dānā ḍāle pūre cār roz ho gaye the.) (Yaśpāl)

5. Present participle ending in -ते (-te): This is used to indicate that a certain amount of time has elapsed since the beginning of the action.

Example:

I have been living in this city for seven years. (*Lit.: 'seven years have happened*)

इस शहर में रहते हुए सात साल हो गए हैं। (is śahar meṃ rahte hue sāt sāl ho gae haiṃ.)

IX. PREFIXES AND SUFFIXES (प्रत्यय PRATYAY)

Students of Hindi who have some knowledge of Sanskrit, and/or Persian or Arabic will often recognize that some Hindi words exist out of different components with an etymology that goes back to one or more of those languages. There are a number of recurrent prefixes and suffixes with their own meaning, helping the student analyze Hindi words in which they are used. Not all compound words have their separate lemma in the dictionary, hence it is helpful to be able to recognize different components in order to derive the meaning of such compound words. Moreover, many compound words can only be found in the dictionary under the prefix with which they start. The following list offers some of the most frequently used pre- and suffixes, followed by a few examples.[1]

IX.1. PREFIXES

Affixes with Perso-Arabic etymology can be found combined with words of Sanskritic origin and vice versa. However, generally the prefixes with Sanskritic origin will be combined with words of Sanskritic origin, while prefixes with Perso-Arabic origin will be attached to words with a Perso-Arabic or Turkish etymology.

IX.1.1. PREFIXES WITH SANSKRITIC ORIGIN

अ- (a-) / अन- (an-) 'un-, anti-, -less'

अभागी (abhāgī) 'unfortunate', अबोल (abol) 'speechless', असुन्दर (asunder) 'ugly' (lit.: anti-beautiful)

अन्तर- (antar-) 'interior', 'inside', 'among'

अन्तर्राष्ट्रीय (antarrāṣṭrīy) 'international' (lit.: 'among nations'), अन्तर्ज्ञान (antarjñān) 'intuition' (lit.: 'inner-knowledge'), अन्तर्मुख (antarmukh) 'introspective' (lit.: 'internal face')

अति- (ati-) 'very much, excessive'

अतिजीवी- (atijīvī-): 'survivor' (lit.: 'very long living'), अतिपातक (atipātak) 'a heinous crime' (lit.: 'excessive sin'), अतिबार (atibār)

1. For a more extensive list, see McGregor, *Outline of Hindi*, 207–215; and Steel, *Hindi Suffixes and Word Formation*, 1–29.

'frequently' (lit.: 'many times'), अतिवाद (ativād) 'extremism' (lit.: 'excessive point of view')

अनु- (anu-) 'after, according to'

अनुमति (anumati-) 'consent, blessing' (lit.: 'according to the feeling, persuasion'), अनुकरण- (anukaraṇ-) imitation (lit.: 'following the making'), अनुताप (anutāp) 'remorse, distress' (lit.: 'after pain, grief')

कु- (ku-) 'bad, defective, ill-'

कुरूप- (kurūp) 'ugly' (lit.: 'of bad appearance, beauty'), कुपुत्र (kuputr) 'bad son', कुचाली (kucālī) 'of bad conduct', कुकर्म (kukarm) 'villainy, sin'; 'a bad action'

दु- (du-) two

दुतरफ़ा (dutarafā) 'having two sides, deceitful', दुभाषिया (dubhāṣiyā) 'interpreter' (lit.: 'speaking two languages'), दुराहा (durāhā) 'a crossroads' (lit.: 'of two roads')

दुश- (duś-) / दुर- (dur-) / दुष- (duṣ-) 'bad, ill-, wrong, difficult'

दुर्भाग्य (durbhāgy) 'misfortune', दुर्वचन (durvacan) 'slander, abuse' (lit.: 'bad speech'), दुर्गम (durgam) 'impassable, difficult to achieve' (lit.: 'difficult to go'), दुश्चलन (duścalan) 'bad conduct', दुष्कर्म (duṣkarm) 'crime, sin'; 'a bad action'

दूर- (dūr-) 'far, remote'

दूरदर्शन (dūrdarśan) television (lit.: 'far seeing, distant observation'), दूरवासी (dūrvāsī) 'outlandish' (lit.: 'living at a distance'). दूरगामी (dūrgāmī) 'far-reaching'

निश- (niś-) / निः (niḥ-) 'without, non-'; 'away; utterly'

निःशंक (niḥśank) 'fearless', निःशक्त (niḥśakt) 'powerless', निःशून्य (niḥśūny) 'vacant' (lit.: 'utterly empty'), नि(ः)शब्द (ni(ḥ)śabd) 'silent, noiseless'

पूर्व- (pūrv-) 'forward, prior, pre-'

पूर्वकल्पना (pūrvkalpnā) 'conjecture, preconceived idea', पूर्वकालिक (pūrvkālik) 'ancient, of former times'

प्रति- (prati-) 're-, counter-, again'

प्रतिकार (pratikār) 'revenge, counteraction', प्रतिजीव (pratijīv) 'antibiotic' (lit.: 'counter-cell, counter–live form'), प्रतिदिन

(pratidin) 'daily', प्रतिफल (pratiphal) 'return, compensation', 'result', प्रतिशंका (pratiśankā), 'constant fear or doubt'

स- (sa-) 'with, along with'

सफल (saphal) 'successful' (lit.: 'with fruit'), सपरिवार (saparivār) 'along with one's family', सहृदय (sahṛday) 'a kindly person' (lit.: 'with heart')

सु- (su-) 'good, well'

सुशीला (suśīlā) 'a woman of good character', सुकर्म (sukarm) 'a good deed', सुचरित (sucarit) 'of good conduct', सुजान (sujān) 'wise, intelligent' (lit.: 'good knowledge, understanding')

IX.1.2. PREFIXES WITH PERSO-ARABIC ORIGIN

ग़ैर- (gair) 'without, un-, not-, in-'

ग़ैरमुमकिन (gairmumkin) 'impossible', ग़ैरमुनासिब (gairmunāsib) 'inappropriate', ग़ैरसरकारी (gairsakārī) 'nongovernmental, private', ग़ैरक़ानूनी (gairqānūnī) 'unlawful, illegal'

न- (na-) / ना- (nā-) 'not, un-, dis-'

नाइनसाफ़ (nā-insāf) 'unjust', नाखुश (nākhuś) 'displeased', नापाक (nāpāk) 'unclean, impure'

ब- (ba-) 'with, upon, by'

बआसानी (ba-āsānī) 'with ease, easily', बज़ोर (bazor) 'by force', बदिल (badil) 'cordially', 'heartily' (lit.: 'by heart'), बदौलत (badaulat) 'by the good fortune of', बहर हाल (bahar-hāl) 'at all events, by all means'

बे- (be-) un-, anti-

बेवक़ूफ़ (bevaqūf) 'ignorant', बेताब (betāb) 'impatient', बेलिहाज़ (belihāz) 'unmindful, unmannerly', बेनसीब (benasīb) 'unfortunate'

फ़ी- (fi-) 'in, per'

फ़ीरूपया (fīrūpayā) 'per rupee', फ़ीसदी (fīsadī) 'percent'

ला- (lā-) 'without, not-'

लाइलाज (lā-ilāj) 'incurable', लाजवाब (lā-javāb) 'without answer, beyond compare', लापरवाह (lā-parvāh) 'thoughtless, indifferent', लापता (lā-patā) 'missing (person)', 'lost (object)' (lit.: 'without trace')

IX.2. SUFFIXES

IX.2.1. NOUNS FORMED FROM VERBAL STEMS

-आई (-āī) (f.)

पढ़ना (paṛhnā) 'to study' > पढ़ाई (paṛhāī) 'a study', सुनना (sunnā) 'to hear' > सुनाई (sunāī) 'hearing', लड़ना (laṛnā) 'to fight' > लड़ाई (laṛāī) 'a fight, battle'

-आन (-ān) (m. and f.)

उड़ना (uṛnā) 'to fly' > उड़ान (uṛān) 'a flight', लगना (lagnā) 'to be imposed (tax)' > लगान (lagān) 'taxation', कटना (kaṭnā) 'to be cut' > कटान (kaṭān) 'a cut'

-आव (-āv) (m.)

घेरना (gernā) 'to encirle, surround' > घेराव (gerāv) 'siege, encirclement', चुनना (cunnā) 'to choose, select' > चुनाव (cunāv) 'election, choice', बचना (bacnā) 'to be saved' > बचाव (bacāv) 'preservation, escape' (from an accident)

-आवट (-āvaṭ) (f.)

रुकना (ruknā) 'to halt' > रुकावट (rukāvaṭ) 'an obstacle', बँधना (baṃdhnā) 'to be tied' > बँधावट (baṃdhāvaṭ) 'a tie, bond'; फुसफुसाना (phusphusānā) 'to whisper' > फुसफुसावट (phusphusāvaṭ) 'a whisper'

-आहट (-āhaṭ) (f.)

मुस्कराना (muskarāna) 'to smile' > मुस्कराहट (muskarāhaṭ) 'a smile', खुजलाना (khujalānā) 'to itch' > खुजलाहट (khujlāhaṭ) 'itchiness', फिसलना (phisalnā) 'to slip' > फिसलाहट (phislāhaṭ) 'slipperiness'

-ऊ (-ū) (m.)

झाड़ना (jhāṛnā) 'to sweep' > झाड़ू (jhāṛū) 'a broom', खिलाना (khilānā) 'to feed' > खिलाऊ (khilāū) 'one who feeds or supports', गँवाना (gaṃvānā) 'to squander, waste' > गँवाऊ (gaṃvāū) 'one who squanders, a waster'

IX.2.2. NOUNS FORMED FROM OTHER NOUNS

-ई (-ī) (m. and f.)

पड़ोस (paṛos) 'neighborhood' > पड़ोसी (paṛosī) 'a neighbor', दोस्त (ḍost) 'friend' > दोस्ती (dostī) 'friendship', नौकर (naukar) '(public) servant' > नौकरी (naukrī) 'service, employment', ग़म (gam) 'grief, sorrow' > ग़मी (gamī) 'time of sorrow: death, mourning'

-पन (-pan) (m.)

बच्चा (baccā) 'child' > बचपन (bacpan) 'childhood', खिलाड़ी (khilāṛī) 'athlete, sportsman' > खिलाड़ीपन (khilāṛīpan) 'sportsmanship', विधवा (vidhvā) 'widow' > विधवापन (vidhvāpan) 'widowhood'

IX.2.3. NOUNS FORMED FROM ADJECTIVES

-ई (-ī) (f.)

बुरा (burā) 'bad' > बुराई (burāī) 'evil', बीमार (bīmār) 'ill' > बीमारी (bīmārī) 'illness', सुन्दर (sundar) 'beautiful' > सुन्दरी (sundarī) 'a beautiful woman'

IX.2.4. AGENT NOUNS FORMED FROM NOUNS

-अक (-ak)

लेख (lekh) 'article' > लेखक (lekhak) 'writer' (m.), विचार (vicār) 'thought, reflection' > विचारक (vicārak) 'thinker', चाल (cāl) 'motion, movement' > चालक (cālak) 'driver'

-इका (-ikā)

लेख (lekh) 'article' > लेखिका (lekhikā) 'writer' (f.), प्रेम (prem) 'love' > प्रमिका (premikā) 'a woman who loves/is loved'

-इया (-iyā)

डाक (ḍāk) 'postal service' > डाकिया (ḍākiyā) 'postman', छल (chal) 'deceit' > छलिया (chaliyā) 'deceiver, a cheat', भेद (bhed) 'secret matter' > भेदिया (bhediyā) 'spy, confidant'

-ई (-ī)

शास्त्र (śāstr) 'science' > शास्त्री (śāstrī) 'scientist, scholar', छल (chal) 'deceit' > छली (chalī) 'deceiver, a cheat', भाग (bhāg) 'share, part' > भागी (bhāgī) 'a partner, shareholder'

-कार (kār)

साहित्य (sāhity) 'literature' > साहित्यकार (sāhityakār) 'writer', कला (kalā) 'art' > कलाकार (kalākār) 'artist', पत्र (patr) 'periodical, journal' > पत्रकार (patrkār) 'journalist'

-दार (dār)

दुकान (dukān) 'shop, store' > दुकानदार (dukāndār) 'shopkeeper', रिश्ता (riśtā) 'relationship, connection' > रिश्तेदार (riśtedār) 'a relative', ज़मीन (zamīn) 'land' > ज़मीनदार (zamīndār) 'landowner, landlord'

IX.2.5. ABSTRACT NOUNS FORMED FROM OTHER NOUNS AND ADJECTIVES

-इयत (-iyat) (f.)

इनसान (insān) 'man, human' > इनसानियत (insāniyat) 'humanity', ख़ास (khās) 'special, distinct' > ख़ासियत (khāsiyat) 'quality, special nature', असल (asl) 'origin, essence' > असलियत (asliyat) 'reality, originality, genuineness'

-ता (-tā) (f.)

वीर (vīr) 'hero' > वीरता (vīrtā) 'heroism', सफल (saphal) 'fruitful' > सफलता (saphaltā) 'fruitfulness, success', सदस्य (sadasy) 'member' > सदस्यता (sadasytā) 'membership', सत्य (saty) 'true, genuine' > सत्यता (satytā) 'the quality of being true, genuine'

-पन (-pan)

अकेला (akelā) 'alone' > अकेलापन (akelāpan) 'loneliness', अंधा (andhā) 'blind' > अंधापन (andhāpan) 'blindness', सीधा (sīdhā) 'direct, correct' > सीधापन (sīdhāpan) 'directness, correctness'

IX.2.6. FEMININE NOUNS FORMED OF MASCULINE NOUNS REFERRING TO ANIMATE BEINGS

-इन (-in)

बाघ (bāgh) 'tiger' > बाघिन (bāghin) 'tigress', मल्लाह (mallāh) 'sailor' > मल्लाहिन (mallāhin) 'a sailor's wife', पड़ोसी (paṛosī) 'neighbor' > पड़ोसिन (paṛosin) 'a female neighbor'

IX.2.7. ADJECTIVES FORMED FROM NOUNS

-इक (-ik)

धर्म (dharm) 'religion' > धार्मिक (dhārmik) 'religious', अधिकार (adhikār) 'authority' > आधिकारिक (ādhikārik) 'having authority, official', इतिहास (itihās) 'history' > ऐतिहासिक (aitihāsik) 'historical'[2]

-ई (-ī)

सुख (sukh) 'happiness' > सुखी (sukhī) 'happy', पर्वत (parvat) 'mountain, hill' > पर्वती (parvatī) 'hilly, mountainous', नियम (niyam)

2. Note that the vowel of the noun will often be lengthened: a > ā; i > ī; u > ū; i, ī, and e > ai; u and ū > o and au; o and ū > au.

'fixed rule, vow, moderation' > नियमी (niyamī) 'following the rules, pious, moderate'

-दार (dār)

ज़िम्मा (zimmā) 'responsibility' > ज़िम्मेदार (zimmedār) 'responsible (for)', समझ (samajh) 'intelligence' > समझदार (samajhdār) 'intelligent', ईमान (īmān) 'honesty, (good) faith' > ईमानदार (īmāndār) 'honest, trustworthy'

IX.2.8. WORDS DERIVED FROM TOPONYMS

-इया (-iyā)

कलकता (kalkatā) 'Kolkata' > कलकतिया (kalkatiyā) 'of or belonging to Kolkata', बम्बाई (bambāī) 'Bombay' > बम्बाईया (bambāīyā) 'of or belonging to Bombay', अमृतसर (amṛtsar) 'Amṛtsar' > अमृतसरिया (amṛtsariyā) 'of or belonging to Amṛtsar'

-ई (-ī)

पंजाब (paṃjāb) 'Punjab' > पंजाबी (paṃjābī) 'Punjabi', गुजरात (gujarāt) 'Gujarat' > गुजराती (gujarātī) 'Gujarati', हिन्द (Hind) '(North) India' > हिन्दी (hindī) 'Hindi'

IX.2.9. DIMINUTIVES (F.)

-अक (-ak)

ढोल (ḍol) 'large drum' > ढोलक (ḍolak) 'small drum', गोल (gol) 'sphere' > गोलक (golak) 'eyeball', सँपुट (saṃpuṭ) 'casket' > सँपुटक (saṃpuṭak) 'small casket'

-आ (ā) > -ई (-ī)

जूता (jūtā) 'shoe' > जूती (jūtī) 'small shoe, slipper, women's shoe', रस्सा (rassā) 'heavy rope' > रस्सी (rassī) 'rope, string', थैला (thailā) 'bag, sack' > थैली (thailī) 'small bag, purse'

-इका (-ikā)

पुस्तक (pustak) 'book' > पुस्तिका (pustikā) 'booklet, brochure' कोश (koś) 'treasury, storeroom' > कोशिका (kośikā) 'biological cell' (lit.: 'small treasury'), तारा (tārā) 'star' > तारिका (tārikā) 'asterisk'

-इया (-iyā)

डिब्बा (ḍibbā) 'box' > डिबिया (ḍibiyā) 'little box', घड़ा (ghaṛā) 'earthen water pot' > घड़िया (ghaṛiyā) 'small earthen pot', चिड़ी (ciṛī) 'bird'

> चिड़िया (ciṛiyā) 'small bird', बेटी (beṭī) 'daughter' > बिटिया (biṭiyā) 'little, dear daughter'[3]

-ईचा (-īcā)

बाग़ (bāg) 'park, large garden' > बाग़ीचा (bāgīcā) 'small garden', ग़ाला (gālā) 'cotton' > ग़ालीचा (gālīcā) 'small carpet'

IX.2.10. ADVERBS FORMED FROM NOUNS

-पूर्वक (-pūrvak)

प्रेम (prem) 'love' > प्रमपूर्वक (prempūrvak) 'lovingly', विश्वास (viśvās) 'trust, confidence' > विश्वासपूर्वक (viśvāspūrvak) 'confidently', अधिकार (adhikār) 'authority' > अधिकारपूर्वक (adhikārpūrvak) 'authoritatively'

Bear in mind that this is only a selection of the wealth of prefixes and suffixes found in Hindi. Note that several prefixes and suffixes, e.g., -ई (-ī) and -दार (dār), can be added to different kinds of words, and depending upon the word they are attached to, they can form either adjectives or nouns.

IX.3. THE SUFFIX -वाला (-VĀLĀ)

IX.3.1. INFINITIVE ON -ने (-NE) + -वाला (-VĀLĀ)

1. Adding the suffix -वाला (-vālā) to an infinitive generates a verbal noun (कर्तृवाचक कृदंत kartṛvācak kṛdant), i.e., a noun to denominate the person who is conducting the action of the verb. E.g., सुननेवाला (sunnevālā) 'the one who does the listening, listener'; रोटी बनानेवाला (roṭī banānevālā) 'the one who makes the roṭīs'; केले बेचनेवाली (kele becnevālī) 'the woman who sells bananas'.

2. Adding the suffix -वाला (-vālā) to an infinitive is used to express that the action is on the verge of happening. E.g., जानेवाली गाड़ी (jānevālī gāṛī) 'the train that is on the verge of leaving'; बोलनेवाली (bolnevālī) 'she who is about to speak'.

---

3. Note that the vowel of the noun will be shortened: a < ā; i < ī; u < ū; i, ī, and e < ai; u and ū < o and au; o and ū < au.

IX.3.2. NOUN + -वाला (-VĀLĀ)

This describes a following noun, whether implicit or explicit in the sentence. This combination can indicate the person who possesses or is connected to something. E.g., दुकानवाला (dukānvālā) 'shopkeeper', पानवाला (pānvālā) 'the seller of betelnut', रिक्षावाला (rikṣāvālā) 'the one who has/drives a rikṣā'.

Example:

The family of the girl fed everybody plenty of pūrīs. (Premcand)

लड़की वालों ने सबको भरपेट पूड़ियाँ खिलाई थीं। (laṛkī vāloṃ ne sabko bharpeṭ pūṛiyāṃ khilāī thīṃ.)

IX.3.3. TOPONYMS + -वाला (-VĀLĀ)

This is used to indicate the inhabitants of that place. E.g., दिल्ली वाला (dillī vālā) 'a (male) resident of Delhi'.

IX.3.4. ADJECTIVE AND ADVERB + -वाला (-VĀLĀ)

This is used to indicate something by a distinguishing characteristic. E.g., लकड़ी वाला (lakṛī vālā) 'the one made of wood', मुझे यह पीली वाली चाहिए। (mujhe yah pīlī vālī cāhie) 'I want the yellow one' (e.g., referring to a *sāṛī*), नज़दीक वाले [डाक-घर] चलें। (nazdīk vāle [dāk-ghar] caleṃ) "To which post office do you want to go?" "Let's go to the nearby one."

IX.4. THE SUFFIX -सा (-SĀ)

The suffix -सा (-sā) acts like an adjective and hence can take the forms -सा (-sā), -से (se), and सी (-sī).

IX.4.1. COMBINED WITH NOUNS AND PRONOUNS

This suffix expresses a comparison.

Examples:

A building like a temple

एक मन्दिर-सी इमारत। (ek mandir-sī imārat)

These children are like monkeys.
वे बच्चे बन्दर-से होते हैं। (ve bacce bandar-se hote haiṃ.)

This ring is like my mother's.
यह अँगूठी मेरी माता जी की-सी है। (yah aṃgūṭhī merī mātā jī kī-sī hai.)

A friend like you
तुम-सा दोस्त। (tum-sā dost)

IX.4.2. COMBINED WITH ADJECTIVES THAT EXPRESS A QUANTITY

The suffix -सा (-sā) can intensify the original meaning or can indicate a certain vagueness.[4]

Examples:

A very high mountain
एक ऊंचा-सा पहाड़ (ek ūṃcā-sā pahāṛ)

A little bit of sugar
थोड़ी-सी चीनी (thoṛī-sī cīnī)

He lives in a very/rather small room.
वह छोटे-से कमरे में रहता है। (vah choṭe-se kamre meṃ rahtā hai.)

Let's take some kind of very light shroud. (Premcand)
कोई हलका-सा क़फ़न ले लें। (koī halkā-sā kafan le leṃ.)

IX.4.3. COMBINED WITH ADJECTIVES EXPRESSING A QUALITY

-सा (-sā) can be used to express a comparison.

Examples:

Bluish water
नीला-सा पानी (nīlā-sā pānī)

4. Kumar, *Hindi for Non-Hindi Speaking People*, 258.

An innocent-looking girl
एक भोली-सी लड़की (ek bholī-sī laṛkī)

Back-breaking labor like that of farmers (Premcand)
किसानों की-सी जाँ-तोड़ मेहनत (kisānoṃ kī-sī jāṃ-toṛ mehnat)

X. REPETITION AND ECHO WORDS

In Hindi, one often comes across reduplication of a word with a hyphen between the two words. This has an intensifying effect, e.g., धीरे-धीरे (dhīre-dhīre) 'very slowly', काला-काला (kālā-kālā) 'pitch black'.

Examples:

[They] inspected different kinds of cloth, silk and cotton, but nothing seemed good. (Premcand)

तरह-तरह के कपड़े, रेशमी और सूती, देखे मगर कुछ जँचा नहीं। (tarah-tarah ke kapṛe, reśmī aur sūtī dekhe, magar kuch jaṃcā nahīṃ.)

Then both started lamenting very loudly and beating their chest. (Premcand)

फिर दोनों ज़ोर-ज़ोर से हाय-हाय करने और छाती पीटने लगे। (phir donoṃ zor-zor se hāy-hāy karne aur chātī pīṭne lage.)

If [I] ask you something, will [you] tell the whole truth? (Varmā)

एक बात पूछूँ सच-सच बतलाओगी? (ek bāt pūchūṃ sac-sac batlāogī?)

With verbs, it gives an intensifying effect, showing variety in the action.

Examples:

After collecting [continuously, from various places] taxes from the poor, where will you keep them safe? (Premcand)

गरीबों का माल बटोर-बटोरकर कहाँ रखोगे। (garībоṃ kā māl baṭor-baṭorkar kahāṃ rakhoge?)

The kind-hearted women from the village kept coming to see the body. (Premcand)

गाँव की नर्म दिल स्त्रियाँ आ-आकर लाश देखती थीं। (gāṃv kī narm dil striyāṃ ā-ākar lāś dekhtī thīṃ.)

Sometimes, the duplication is not exact, and the second word begin with a different letter (often the v-). In such a reduplication, creating a sound game is the aim. The second word generally does not exist on its own and just echoes the first word. E.g., चहल-पहल (cahal-pahal) 'festivity', आम-वाम (ām-vām) 'mango and the like', चाय-वाय (cāy-vāy) 'tea and stuff', पिक्चर-विक्चर (pikcar-vikcar) 'a movie',[1] खाना-शाना (khānā-sānā) 'food', आग-वाग (āg-vāg) 'fires and the like'.[2] A vowel change can occur instead: ठीक-ठाक (ṭhīk-ṭhāk) 'good'.

Example:

Here, people started to cut bamboo and such. (Premcand)

इधर लोग बाँस-वाँस काटने लगे। (idhar log bāṃs-vāṃs kāṭne lage.)

Moreover, one can come across a combination of two words that are neither reduplications nor echo words, but antonyms. This indicates either a span or a variety of a category, e.g., झूठ-सच (jhūṭh-sac) 'lie-truth', hence 'misrepresentation, fabrication'; छोटे-बड़े (choṭe-baṛe) 'small-big', 'young-old', hence 'varied, various', कीड़े-मकौड़े (kīṛe-makauṛe): 'worms-large insects', hence 'various insects and insect-related animals'.

---

1. Bismillāh, *Athiti devo bhav*, 143.
2. Bismillāh, *ṭinnū kā ṭelifon*, 130.

XI. NUMBERS (संख्या SAṂKHYĀ)

XI.1. CARDINAL NUMBERS (गणन संख्याएँ GAṆAN SAṂKHYĀEṂ)

० (0)	शून्य, सिफ़र	(śūny), (sifr)
१ (1)	एक	(ek)
२ (2)	दो	(do)
३ (3)	तीन	(tīn)
४ (4)	चार	(cār)
५ (5)	पाँच	(pāṃc)
६ (6)	छः	(chaḥ)[1]
७ (7)	सात	(sāt)
८ (8)	आठ	(āṭh)
९ (9)	नौ	(nau)
१० (10)	दस	(das)
२० (20)	बीस	(bīs)
३० (30)	तीस	(tīs)
४० (40)	चालीस	(cālīs)
५० (50)	पचास	(pacās)
६० (60)	साठ	(sāṭh)
७० (70)	सत्तर	(sattar)
८० (80)	अस्सी	(assī)
९० (90)	नव्वे	(navve)[2]
१०० (100)	सौ	(sau)

See the appendix for the numbers from 1 to 100.

For numbers over one hundred, the different cardinals are placed one after the other.

१०१ (101)	एक सौ एक	(ek sau ek)
१३४ (134)	एक सौ छत्तीस	(ek sau chattīs)
४०० (400)	चार सौ	(cār sau)
८७९ (879)	आठ सौ उन्नासी	(āṭh sau unnāsī)

1. Also छह (chah) (the pronunciation of both is 'che') or sometimes even छै (chai).
2. Also नब्बे (nabbe).

Note the following round numbers.

१००० (1,000)	एक हज़ार	(ek hazār)
१०० ००० (100,000)	एक लाख	(ek lākh)
१ ००० ००० (1,000,000)	नियुत	(niyut)
१० ००० ००० (10,000,000)	एक करोड़	(ek karoṛ)

For numbers between one hundred thousand and ten million, numbers are counted in multiples of one hundred thousand. For numbers over ten million, multiples of ten million are used. The word नियुत (niyut) 'million' is hardly ever used. It mainly means 'a large number' and is sometimes also translated as '100,000'.

Examples:

1,500,000	पन्द्रह लाख (pandrah lākh) (15 × 100,000)
80,380,023	आठ करोड़ तीन लाख अस्सी हज़ार तेईस (āṭh karoṛ tīn lākh assī hazār teīs) (8 × 10 million, 3 × 100,000, 80 × 1000, 23 × 1)
15,530,500	एक करोड़ पचपन लाख तीस हज़ार पाँच सौ (ek karoṛ pacpan lākh tīs hazār pāṃc sau) (1 × 10 million, 55 × 100,000, 30 × 1000, 5 × 100)

XI.2. FRACTIONS (भिन्न BHINN)

For the numbers 0.5, 1.5, 2.5, a quarter less and a quarter more, Hindi has separate words. These are used in combination with numbers for prices, but also when telling time or talking about weight.

आधा (ādhā)	a half
डेढ़ (ḍeṛh)	1.5, e.g., डेढ़ सौ रुपये (ḍeṛh sau rupaye) '150 Rs' डेढ़ बजे (ḍeṛh baje) '1:30'
ढाई (ḍhāī)	2.5, e.g., ढाई सौ रुपये (ḍhāī sau rupaye) '250 Rs' ढाई बजे (ḍhāī baje) '2:30'
साढ़ (sāṛhe)	one half more of the unit one is counting in, added to numbers over 2 साढ़े चार (sāṛhe cār) '4.5'

	साढ़े पाँच सौ रुपये (sāṛhe pāṃc sau rupaye) '550 Rs'
	साढ़े तीन बजे (sāṛhe tīn baje) '3:30'
पौने (paune)	one quarter less of the unit one is counting in, added to numbers 2 and over
	पौने दो (paune do) '1¾'
	पौने दो बजे (paune do baje) '1:45'
	पौने दो के.जी. (paune do ke.gī.) '1 kg 750 g'
सवा (savā)	one quarter more of the unit one is counting in, added to numbers 2 and over
	सवा दो (savā do) '2¼'
	सवा दो बजे (savā do baje) '2:15'
	सवा दो के.जी. (savā do ke. jī.) '2 kg 250 g'

XI.3. ORDINAL NUMBERS (क्रमसूचक संख्याएँ KRAMASŪCAK SAṂKHYĀEṂ)

The ordinals from one through six are irregular.

first	पहला (pahlā)
second	दूसरा (dūsrā)
third	तीसरा (tīsrā)
fourth	चौथा (cauthā)
fifth	पाँचवाँ (pāṃcvāṃ)
sixth	छठा / छठवाँ (chaṭhā / chaṭhvāṃ)

From seven onward, the cardinal numbers follow the pattern of पाँचवाँ (pāṃcvāṃ) 'fifth'. The suffix -वाँ (vāṃ) is simply added to the cardinal, e.g., तेरहवाँ (terahvāṃ) 'thirteenth'. All ordinal numbers follow the declension of adjectives, e.g., 'fourth': nom. m. sg. चौथा (cauthā); f. sg./pl. चौथी (cauthī); m. pl./m.obl. sg. चौथे (cauthe).

Ordinals ending in -वाँ (vāṃ) retain their nasalization, e.g., 'thirteenth': तेरहवाँ (terahvāṃ), तेरहवीं (terahvīṃ), तेरहवें (terahveṃ).

XI.4. COLLECTIVES (समूहवाचक SAMŪHVĀCAK)

Collectives are words that are used in the singular to indicate a group. The noun itself stays singular, while the adjectives and verbs that agree with it in gender are put in plural.

Cardinals that end in -ों (oṃ) are also collectives, e.g., चारों (cāroṃ) 'all four', दोनों (donoṃ) 'both'. The number one hundred has a special form: सैकड़ों (saikṛoṃ) 'hundreds'.

One frequently comes across pairs of numbers with a hyphen in between. This is used to give a number by approximation. Moreover, one will often encounter "couples" of numbers (not in sequence or numerological order) connected by a hyphen. This is used to indicate a number by approximation, e.g., दो-चार (do-cār) 'two to four', दस-पाँच (das-pāṃc) 'five to ten'.

Sometimes, the number one एक (ek) is added to another number, without a hyphen in between. This means 'about', e.g., दो एक (do ek) 'about two' or 'very few', पच्चीस एक (paccīs ek) 'about 25'.

Example:

You must have eaten about twenty pūrīs. (Premchand)
तुमने एक बीस पूरियाँ खाई होंगी। (tumne ek bīs pūriyāṃ khāī hoṃgī.)

When the number one, एक (ek), is combined with a noun in the plural, this indicates a category or group.

Example from Yaśpāl:

One class of prostitutes lives in Cāvṛī Bāzār.
एक रंडियाँ रहती हैं चावड़ी में। (ek raṇḍiyāṃ rahtī haiṃ cāvṛī meṃ.)

XII. TIME AND CALENDARS: ERAS, SEASONS, MONTHS, DAYS, HOURS, AND MINUTES

XII.1. ERAS

The following calendars are mainly used for religious purposes. In everyday life, the Western calendar is generally used.

XII.1.1. HINDU

The Hindu calendar is a lunar calendar when it comes to months, but the lunar months fit into a solar year. The Hindu era (संवत्, sanvat) is called विक्रमादित्य (vikramādity) or विक्रम (vikram), started by the king bearing the same name in 57–56 B.C. (ई.पू. (ī.pū.)). To convert a date from Vikram to the Gregorian calendar, subtract 56 from the Vikram year if the date is situated between चैत (cait) and the first half of पूस (pūs). For dates between the second half of पूस (pūs) and the month of फागुन (phāgun), subtract 57.

XII.1.2. ISLAMIC

The Islamic calendar is a purely lunar calendar, both for months and years. Six months consist of thirty days, six months of twenty-nine days. A lunar year is thus shorter than a solar year. The Islamic calendar, beginning its count in A.D. 622, is called Hijri. To convert a Hijri date to the Gregorian calendar, use the following formula:

(Hijri year × 0.970225) + 621.54

To convert from the Gregorian to Hijri calendar:[1]

(Gregorian year – 621.54) / 0.970225

For exact conversions, one has to use conversion tables.

1. Thackston, *Koranic and Classical Arabic*, 249–250.

XII.2. SEASONS AND MONTHS

XII.2.1. HINDU

A Hindu solar year (i.e., a year having a fixed duration) consists of six seasons. Every season consists of two lunar months that each start around the middle of the Gregorian months.

A lunar month consists of two periods of fifteen moon days, तिथि (tithi); the first half of the month starts with the new moon. This period, known as the waxing moon, is called शुक्ल पक्ष (śukl pakṣ)/सुदि (sudi)/सुदी (sudī). The second half of the month starts with the full moon and is called कृष्ण पक्ष (kṛṣṇ pakṣ)/बदी (badī), or waning moon.

The six seasons and the names of the Hindu months follow. The first name is the Hindi name, while the second is the Sanskrit name, used in more formal contexts.

Spring:

बसंत (basant) consists of चैत (cait) or चैत्र (caitr) (March–April)
and
बेसाख (besākh) or वैशाख (vaiśākh) (April–May)

Summer:[2]

ग्रीष्म (grīṣm) consists of जेठ (jeṭh) or ज्येष्ठ (jyeṣṭh) (May–June)
and
असाढ़ (asāṛh) or आषाढ़ (āṣāṛh) (June–July)

Rainy season:

वर्षा* (varṣā) consists of सावन (sāvan) or श्रावण (śrāvaṇ) (July–August)
and
भादों (bhādoṃ) and भाद्रपद (bhādrapad) (August–September)

Autumn:

शरद* (śarad) consists of क्वार (kvār) or आश्विन (āśvin) (September–October)

2. Also गरमी (garmī).

and
कातिक (kātik) or कार्त्तिक (kārttik) (October–November)

Winter:[3]

हेमंत (hemant) consists of अगहन (agahan) or आग्रहायण (āgrahāyaṇ) (November–December)
and
पूस (pūs) or पौष (pauṣ) (December–January)

Cold season:

शिशिर (śiśir) consists of माघ (māgh) or माघ (māgha) (January–February)
and
फागुन (phāgun) or फाल्गुन (phālgun) (February–March)[4]

Approximately every thirty-two months, an intercalary month is added to neutralize the discrepancy between the length of the lunar months and the solar year. This intercalary month is called मलमास (malmās) or अधिकमास (adhikmās).

XII.2.2. ISLAMIC

The year starts with the month of Muḥarram, which moves forward every year when compared to the Western calendar. The names of the other months are Safar, Rabī'-al-awwal, Rabī'-al-ā<u>kh</u>ir, Jumādā'l ūlā, Jumādā'l u<u>kh</u>rā, Rajab, Śa'bān, Ramazān, Śawwāl, Zū'l qa'dah, and Zū'l ḥijjah.

XII.2.3. EVERYBODY

Basically, everybody uses the Western calendar nowadays. The Christian era is called ईसवी सन (īsvī san). The names of the months are the same as the names in the Western calendar, but with a Hindi

3. Also जाड़ा (jāṛā) / सरदी (sardī).
4. All seasons and months are masculine words, except for those marked with an asterisk.

pronunciation: जनवरी (janvarī), फ़रवरी (farvarī), मार्च (mārc), अप्रैल (aprail), मई (maī), जून (jūn), जुलाई (julāī), अगस्त (agast), सितम्बर (sitambar), अक्तूबर (aktūbar), नवम्बर (navambar), दिसम्बर (disambar).

XII.3. DAYS

Usually, the days of the week are the same for everybody.

Monday	सोमवार (somvār) or पीर (pīr)
Tuesday	मंगलवार (maṃgalvār)
Wednesday	बुधवार (budhvār)
Thursday	गुरुवार (guruvār)/बृहस्पतिवार (bṛhaspativār) or जुमारात (jumārāt)/जुमेरात (jumerāt)
Friday	शुक्रवार (śukrvār) or जुमा (juma)
Saturday	शनिवार (śanivār) or सनीचर (sanīcar)
Sunday	रविवार (ravivār) or इतवार (itvār)

Notes:

1. The component -वार (-vār) is often dropped in colloquial Hindi, as well as in Urdu.

2. The words जुमारात (jumārāt)/जुमेरात (jumerāt) for Thursday, जुमा (juma) for Friday, and पीर (pīr) for Monday are generally used by Urdu speakers and Muslim Hindi speakers.

XII.4. HOURS AND MINUTES

XII.4.1. BASIC TERMINOLOGY

घण्टा (ghaṇṭā) 'an hour'
बजना (bajnā) 'to sound, to strike'

Hence, बजा (bajā)/ बजे (baje) 'to mark an hour'

XII.4.2. ON THE HOUR

Examples:

एक बजा (ek bajā) 'one o'clock'

एक बजा है (ek bajā hai) 'it is one o'clock'

एक बजे (ek baje) 'at one o'clock'

दो बजे (do baje) 'two o'clock'

दो बजे हैं (do baje haiṃ) 'it is two o'clock'

XII.4.3. HALF PAST THE HOUR

साढ़े (sāṛhe) 'plus a half'
डेढ़[5] (ḍeṛh) 'one and a half (times)'

Examples:

डेढ़ बजा (ḍeṛh bajā) '1:30'

डेढ़ बजे (ḍeṛh baje) 'at 1:30'

डेढ़ बजा है (ḍeṛh bajā hai) 'it is 1:30' (grammatically singular!)

ढाई (ḍhāī) 'two and a half (times)'

Examples:

ढाई बजे (ḍhāī baje) '(at) 2:30'[6]

ढाई बजे हैं (ḍhāī baje haiṃ) 'it is 2:30'

साढ़े तीन बजे (sāṛhe tīn baje) '(at) 3:30'

साढ़े तीन बजे हैं (sāṛhe tīn baje haiṃ) 'it is 3:30'

XII.4.4. QUARTER PAST AND QUARTER TO

Fifteen minutes before the hour

पौन (paun) (also 'पौना' (paunā))/पौने (paune) 'a quarter less (¾)'

Examples:

पौन बजा (paun bajā) '12:45'

पौन बजा है (paun bajā hai) 'it is 12:45'

पौन बजे (paun baje) 'at 12:45'

पौने दो बजे (paune do baje) '(at) 1:45'

पौने दो बजे हैं (paun do baje haiṃ) 'it is 1:45'

---

5. Grammatically, this is singular. Hence डेढ़ बजा है (ḍeṛh bajā hai) and not डेढ़ बजे हैं (ḍeṛh baje haiṃ).
6. The "at" is put between brackets, because को (ko) as an indication of time can be dropped and the oblique will in such cases be retained.

Fifteen minutes after the hour

सवा (savā) 'plus a quarter (one and a quarter)'

Examples:

सवा बजा (savā bajā) '1:15'

सवा बजा है (savā bajā hai) 'it is 1:15'

सवा बजे (savā baje) 'at 1:15'

सवा दो बजे (savā do baje) '(at) 2:15'[7]

सवा दो बजे हैं (savā do baje haiṃ) 'it is 2:15'

XII.4.5. TO THE MINUTE

Minutes to the hour

बजने में (bajne meṃ)

Examples:

पाँच बजने में बीस मिनट[8] (pāṃc bajne meṃ bīs minaṭ) '4:40'

पाँच बजने में बीस मिनट बाक़ी हैं (pāṃc bajne meṃ bīs minaṭ bāqī haiṃ) 'it is 4:40' ('बाक़ी' (bāqī) means 'left over, remaining')

पाँच बजने से बीस मिनट पहले (pāṃc bajne meṃ bīs minaṭ pahle) 'at 4:40'

Minutes past the hour

बजकर (bajkar) absolutive of बजना (bajnā)

Examples:

पाँच बजकर पच्चीस मिनट (pāṃc bajkar paccīs minaṭ) '5:25'

पाँच बजकर पच्चीस मिनट हुए हैं (pāṃc bajkar paccīs minaṭ hue haiṃ) 'it is 5:25'

पाँच बजकर पच्चीस मिनट पर (pāṃc bajkar paccīs minaṭ par) 'at 5:25'

---

7. The "at" is put between brackets, because को as an indication of time can be dropped and the oblique will in such a cases be retained.
8. The spelling मिणट (miṇaṭ) is used as well.

XII.5. SPECIFYING THE MOMENT OF THE DAY

Ancient Sanskrit scriptures show us that in ancient times, the day was divided into eight watches of three hours. There are still remnants from this system in Hindi through the use of the word **पहर** (pahar) 'a watch of three hours'.

दोपहर (dopahar) 'midday (the end of the second watch)'
तीसरा पहर (tīsrā pahar) 'the early afternoon'
दोपहर के बाद (dopahar ke bād) 'in the afternoon'
पहर रात (को) (pahar rāt (ko)) 'late in the night'
आठों पहर (āṭhoṃ pahar) 'the entire 24 hours of a day'

One the other hand, the day is also divided into four periods:

सुबह (subah) 'in the morning (from 6 a.m. to 11 a.m.)'
दिन (din) 'the day (from 11 a.m. to 3 or 4 p.m.)'
शाम (śām) 'evening (from 3 or 4 p.m. to 9 p.m.)'
रात (rāt) 'night (from 9 p.m. to 6 a.m.)'

For these indications of time, the postpositions को (ko) and के (ke) can be used, but are often dropped. However, when dropped, the oblique case is still used.

Examples:

At 5 a.m.:

रात को पाँच बजे (rāt ko pāṃc baje)

रात पाँच बजे (rāt pāṃc baje)

पाँच बजे रात को (pāṃc baje rāt ko)

रात के पाँच बजे (rāt ke pāṃc baje)

Appendix

Cardinal numbers 1–100

1	१ एक	ek
2	२ दो	do
3	३ तीन	tīn
4	४ चार	cār
5	५ पाँच	pāṃc
6	६ छः	chaḥ
7	७ सात	sāt
8	८ आठ	āṭh
9	९ नौ	nau
10	१० दस	das
11	११ ग्यारह	gyārah
12	१२ बारह	bārah
13	१३ तेरह	terah
14	१४ चौदह	caudah
15	१५ पन्द्रह	pandrah
16	१६ सोलह	solah
17	१७ सत्रह	satrah
18	१८ अटारह	aṭārah
19	१९ उन्नसि	unnīs
20	२० बीस	bīs
21	२१ इक्कीस	ikkīs
22	२२ बाईस	bāīs
23	२३ तेईस	teīs
24	२४ चौबीस	caubīs
25	२५ पच्चीस	paccīs
26	२६ छब्बीस	chabbīs
27	२७ सत्ताईस	sattāīs
28	२८ अट्ठाईस	aṭṭhāīs
29	२९ उनतीस	untīs
30	३० तीस	tīs
31	३१ इकतीस	iktīs
32	३२ बत्तीस	battīs
33	३३ तेंतीस	teṃtīs
34	३४ चौंतीस	cauṃtīs
35	३५ पैंतीस	paiṃtīs
36	३६ छत्तीस	chattīs
37	३७ सैंतीस	saiṃtīs
38	३८ अड़तीस	aṛtīs
39	३९ उनतालीस	untālīs
40	४० चालीस	cālīs
41	४१ इकतालीस	iktālīs
42	४२ बयालीस	bayālīs
43	४३ तेंतालीस	teṃtālīs
44	४४ चवालीस	cavālīs
45	४५ पैंतालीस	paiṃtālīs
46	४६ छियालीस	chiyālīs
47	४७ सैंतालीस	saiṃtālīs
48	४८ अड़तालीस	aṛtālīs
49	४९ उनचास	uncās
50	५० पचास	pacās
51	५१ इकावन	ikāvan[1]
52	५२ बावन	bāvan
53	५३ तिरपन	tirpan
54	५४ चौवन	cauvan

1. Also इक्यावन ikyāvan.

55	५५ पचपन	pacpan	78	७८ अठहत्तर	aṭhhattar
56	५६ छप्पन	chappan	79	७९ उन्नासी	unnāsī[2]
57	५७ सत्तावन	sattāvan	80	८० अस्सी	assī
58	५८ अट्ठावन	aṭṭhāvan	81	८१ इक्यासी	ikyāsī[3]
59	५९ उनसठ	unsaṭh	82	८२ बयासी	bayāsī
60	६० साठ	sāṭh	83	८३ तिरासी	tirāsī
61	६१ इकसठ	iksaṭh	84	८४ चौरासी	caurāsī
62	६२ बासठ	bāsaṭh	85	८५ पचासी	pacāsī
63	६३ तिरसठ	tirsaṭh	86	८६ छियासी	chiyāsī
64	६४ चौंसठ	cauṃsaṭh	87	८७ सत्तासी	sattāsī
65	६५ पैंसठ	paiṃsaṭh	88	८८ अट्ठासी	aṭṭhāsī
66	६६ छियासठ	chiyāsaṭh	89	८९ नवासी	navāsī
67	६७ सरसठ	sarsaṭh	90	९० नव्वे	navve[4]
68	६८ अड़सठ	aṛsaṭh	91	९१ इकानवे	ikānve[5]
69	६९ उनहत्तर	unhattar	92	९२ बानवे	bānve
70	७० सत्तर	sattar	93	९३ तिरानवे	tirānve
71	७१ इकहत्तर	ik-hattar	94	९४ चौरानवे	caurānve
72	७२ बहत्तर	bahattar	95	९५ पचानवे	pacānve
73	७३ तिहत्तर	tihattar	96	९६ छियानवे	chiyānve
74	७४ चौहत्तर	cauhattar	97	९७ सत्तानवे	satānve
75	७५ पचहत्तर	pac-hattar	98	९८ अट्ठानवे	aṭṭhānve
76	७६ छिहत्तर	chihattar	99	९९ निनानवे	ninānave[6]
77	७७ सतहत्तर	sat-hattar	100	१०० सौ	sau

2. Also उन्यासी unyāsī.
3. Also इकासी ikāsī.
4. Also नब्बे nabbe.
5. Also इक्यानवे ikyānve.
6. Also निन्यान्वे ninyānve.

References

Agnihotri, Rama Kant. *Hindi: An Essential Grammar*. London: Routledge, 2007.

Bhata, Tej K. *A History of the Hindi Grammatical Tradition: Hindi-Hindustani Grammar, Grammarians, History, and Problems*. Leiden: E. J. Brill, 1987.

Bismillāh, Abdul. *Atithi devo bhav*. Dillī: Rājkamal Prakāśan, 1990.

Bureau of Education. "Minute by the Hon'ble T. B. Macaulay, dated the 2nd February 1835." In *Selections from Educational Records, Part I (1781–1839)*, ed. H. Sharp, 107–117. Calcutta: Superintendent, Government Printing, 1920. Repr. Delhi: National Archives of India, 1965. http://www.columbia.edu/itc/mealac/pritchett/00generallinks/macaulay/txt_minute_education_1835.html.

Critical Language Scholarship Program. "CLS Hindi." Accessed November 15, 2015. http://www.clscholarship.org/languages/hindi.

Das, Pradeep Kumar. *Grammatical Agreement in Hindi-Urdu and Its Major Varieties*. Munich: Lincom Europa, 2006.

Davison, Alice. "On the Form and Meaning of Hindi Passive Sentences." *Lingua* 58 (1982): 149–179.

———. "Peculiar Passives." *Language* 56, no. 1 (1980): 42–66.

Despande, Madhav M. "Efforts to Vernacularize Sanskrit: Degree of Success and Failure." In *Handbook of Language and Ethnic Identity; The Success-Failure Continuum in Language and Ethnic Identity Efforts, Volume 2*, ed. J. A. Fishman and O. Garcia, 218–229. Oxford: Oxford University Press, 2011.

Ethnologue: Languages of the World. Accessed September 18, 2013. http://www.ethnologue.com.

Ethnologue: Languages of the World. "Hindi." Accessed November 5, 2015. https://www.ethnologue.com/language/hin.

Ethnologue: Languages of the World. "Urdu." Accessed November 5, 2015. https://www.ethnologue.com/language/urd.

Everaert, Christine. *Tracing the Boundaries between Hindi and Urdu: Lost and Added in Translation between 20th Century Short Stories*. Brill's Indological Library 32. Leiden: Brill, 2010.

Government of India. "The Constitution of India 1949: Central Government Act: Article 343." Accessed October 22, 2015. http://indiankanoon.org/doc/379861/.

Government of India, Ministry of Home Affairs. "Census of India 2001: Abstract of Speakers' Strength of Languages and Mother Tongues—2001." Accessed November 10, 2015. http://www.censusindia.gov.in/%28S%282scoev45b4mhlg45mz5jq345%29%29/Census_Data_2001/Census_Data_Online/Language/Statement1.aspx.

———. "Census of India 2011: Data Highlights." Accessed November 10, 2015. http://www.censusindia.gov.in/Ad_Campaign/press/DataHighlghts.pdf.

Government of Pakistan. "The Constitution of Pakistan: Part XII: Chapter 4: General [Articles 248–259]." Accessed November 28, 2015. http://www.pakistani.org/pakistan/constitution/part12.ch4.html.

Gulzār. *Rāvī pār aur anya kahāniyāṃ*. Mumba'ī: Rupa and Co., 1999.

Hautli-Janisz, Annette. "Urdu/Hindi Motion Verbs and Their Implementation in a Lexical Resource." Doctoral diss., Universität Konstanz, 2014. http://kops.uni-konstanz.de/handle/123456789/28820.

Hook, Peter. *The Compound Verb in Hindi*. Ann Arbor: Center for South and Southeast Asian Studies, University of Michigan, 1974.

———. *Hindi Structures Intermediate Level*. Ann Arbor: Center for South and Southeast Asian Studies, University of Michigan, 1979.

———. *Hindi Structures: Intermediate Level, with Drills, Exercises, and Key*. Michigan Papers on South and Southeast Asia. Ann Arbor: Center for South and Southeast Asian Studies, University of Michigan, 1999.

Jain, Usha. *Advanced Hindi Grammar*. Berkeley, CA: Center for South Asia Studies, 2007.

———. *Introduction to Hindi Grammar*. Berkeley, CA: Centers for South and Southeast Asia Studies, 1995.

Kachru, Yamuna. *Aspects of Hindi Grammar*. New Delhi: Manohar Publications, 1980.

———. *An Introduction to Hindi Syntax*. Urbana: Department of Linguistics, University of Illinois, 1966.

Kellogg, Samuel H. *A Grammar of the Hindi Language*. 1876. Repr., London: Routledge and Kegan Paul, 1933.

———. *A Grammar of the Hindí Language: In Which Are Treated the High Hindí, Braj, and the Eastern Hindí of the Rámáyan of Tulsi Dás, also the Colloquial Dialects of Rájputáná, Kumáon, Avadh, Ríwá, Bhojpúr, Magadha, Maithila, etc., with Copious Philological Notes*, 3rd ed. 1938. Repr., London: Routledge and Kegan Paul, 1955.

Koul, Omkar N., ed. *Topics in Hindi Linguistics*. Vol. 2. New Delhi: Bahri Publications, 1981.

Kumar, Kavita. *Hindi for Non-Hindi Speaking People*. 2nd ed. New Delhi: Rupa and Company, 1997.

Masica, Colin P. *The Indo-Aryan Languages*. Cambridge Language Surveys. Cambridge: Cambridge University Press, 1991.

McGregor, Ronald Stuart. *Outline of Hindi Grammar*. 1972. 3rd rev. ed., Oxford: Oxford University Press, 1995.

———. *The Oxford Hindi-English Dictionary*. Oxford: Oxford University Press, 1993.

Montaut, Annie. *A Grammar of Hindi*. Munich: Lincom Europa, 2005.

———. "The Rise of Non-Canonical Subjects and Semantic Alignments in Hindi." *Studies in Language Companion Series* 140, no. 1 (2013): 91–117.

https://halshs.archives-ouvertes.fr/halshs-00962420/file/Montaut_Non_canonical_subjects.pdf.
Platts, John T. *Dictionary of Urdu, Classical Hindi, and English*. 1884. Repr., Delhi: Munshiram Manoharlal, 1984.
———. *A Grammar of the Hindustani or Urdu Language*. 1873. Repr., Delhi: Munshiram Manoharlal, 1990.
Pollock, Sheldon. *The Language of the Gods in the World of Men: Sanskrit, Culture, and Power in Premodern India*. Berkeley: University of California Press, 2006.
Prasad, K. V. S., and Virk, Shafqat Mumtaz. "Computational Evidence That Hindi and Urdu Share a Grammar but Not the Lexicon." In *Proceedings of the 3rd workshop on South and Southeast Asian Natural Language Processing (SANLP), COLING, Mumbai* (December 2012): 1–14. http://www.aclweb.org/anthology/W12-5001.
Premcand. *Mānsarovar 1*. 8 vols. Ilāhābād: Sarasvatī Press, 1965.
Rākeś, Mohan. *Mohan rākeś kī sampurṇ kahāniyāṃ*. Dillī: Rājpāl, 1999.
Sandahl, Stella. *A Hindi Reference Grammar*. Leuven: Peters, 2000.
Scharpé, Adriaan. *Handleiding bij de studie van het Klassieke Sanskrit*. Leuven: Vlaamsche Drukkerij, 1943.
Schmidt, Ruth Laila. *Urdu: An Essential Grammar*. London: Routledge, 1999.
SIL International. "Scriptsource: Devanagari (Nagari)." Accessed December 1, 2015. http://scriptsource.org/cms/scripts/page.php?item_id=script_detail&key=Deva.
Snell, R. "A List of Common Expressions Featuring the Postposition *ko*." Hindi Urdu Flagship. Austin, TX. Accessed December 8, 2015. http://hindiurduflagship.org/assets/pdf/Hindi_Ko.pdf.
Snell, R., and S. Weightman. *Teach Yourself Hindi*. London: Hodder and Stoughton, 1989.
Steel, Brian. *Hindi Suffixes and Word Formation*. 2013. Accessed December 19, 2015. http://briansteel.net/writings/india/bsteelhindi3_suffixes.pdf.
Thackston, Wheeler M. *An Introduction to Koranic and Classical Arabic*. Bethesda, MD: Ibex Publishers, 1994.
Ugra, Pāṇḍey Bacan Śarma. *Aisī holī khelo lāl*. Dillī: Ātmārām eṇḍ sanz, 1993.
Varmā, Bhagavatīcaraṇ. *Merī priy kahāniyāṃ*. Dillī: Rājpāl eṇḍ sanz, 1980.
Versteegh, Kees. *The Arabic Language*. New York: Colombia University Press, 1993.
Yaśpāl. *Yaśpāl kī sampūrṇ kahāniyāṃ*. Illāhābād: Lokbhāratī Prakāśan, 2000.

Index

ability, 126, 133
absolutive, 72, 167; adverbial, 90–91; formation, 74, 89; for sequential actions, 89–91; for simultaneous actions, 91; with vector verb, 111
abugida alphabet, 21
accusative case, 33–35; direct objects, 34–37, 68, 77–80, 104, 116; time and place indications, 33–34, 40–42, 76–80
actions: with certain duration, 118–119, 128, 129; completed, 75–77, 84n.9, 111, 117, 119, 126, 135, 144; consecutive, 89–91; expressing inability, 121, 126, 133; frequent/habitual, 75, 101, 114; incomplete, 74, 135; through intermediary, 104–110, 120; with lasting effect, 128–129; ongoing, 84, 119–120, 135, 139; passive, 120–121; simultaneous, 91; sudden, 123–125
addressing, 59, 73n.2; close relationships, 51, 92; God, 92; groups, 31–32, 93; peers, 52; subordinates, 50–51, 92; superiors, 51, 92–93
adjectives, 7, 31, 39, 49, 54, 65, 67, 82; in comparisons, 62–63; declension, 48; interrogative, 57–59; invariable, 48–49; participles as, 135, 137–138, 140–141; possessive pronoun as, 38–39, 42, 50–52; in word formation, 149–150, 152–154, 160
adjuncts: causal/conditional, 37–38; instrumental, 37–38, 105; locative, 33–34, 40–42; temporal, 33–34, 40–42, 76–80
adverbs: absolutive as, 90–91; in comparisons, 62–63; in compound postpositions, 42–43; in expressions of time, 34; participles as, 135, 138–141; in word formation, 152–153
agreement of verbs: with direct object, 79–80; infinitives, 69–70, 80, 115–116, 126; perfective tense, 78–80
alphabet: alphasyllabary, 21; aspirates, 19–20; consonants, 15–20; fricatives, 19; liquids or semi-vocals, 18; nasals, 15–17; occlusive or plosives, 15–17; variants on basic letters, 20–21; vowels, 13–14
ambitransitive verbs, 105
ānā, 66–67, 83, 109, 111–113
animate objects, 34–36, 79, 150
anunāsik, 25
anusvār, 25
apnā, 50–51
Arabic, 3, 5–6, 8, 20; Arabicized, 5–6; Perso-Arabic, 7–9, 20, 46, 145, 147
articulation: place and mode, 15, 25
aspirated, 16
aspirates, 19–20, 26; omission of, 22n.3, 26
auxiliary verbs. *See* vector verbs

baiṭhnā, 83, 127–128
Bollywood, 7
British: Crown, 6; government, 7; Raj, 6

cāhie, 69–71, 83, 97, 115–116
cāhnā, 83, 115
calendar, 162–165; conversion to Gregorian, 162; Hindu, 162–163; Islamic, 162, 164
can (ability), 126, 133
candrabindu, 25; candra, 26
cardinal numbers, 158–159, 169–170
cases, 4; ablative, 40–41; accusative, 33–34, 38, 40–42; dative, 40–41; genitive, 38–40, 50–52; instrumental, 37–38, 105; locative, 33–34, 38, 40–42; nominative, 31–32, 35–36, 38–39, 45–46, 48, 160; oblique, 22, 26, 31–35, 36–44, 45–46, 48, 50–52, 78, 135, 137, 139, 160, 166–168; of personal pronouns, 50–51; vocative, 31–32, 45, 48
causative, 104–106, 109–110; alternative formation, 107–108; with combined

About the Author

Christine Everaert is an assistant professor of Hindi-Urdu at the University of Utah in Salt Lake City. She was inspired to write this grammar after teaching Hindi and Urdu for more than a decade. Her research focuses on Hindi and Urdu short story literature and linguistics. She is the author of *Tracing the Boundaries between Hindi and Urdu: Lost and Added in Translation between 20th Century Short Stories.*